Metamorphosis

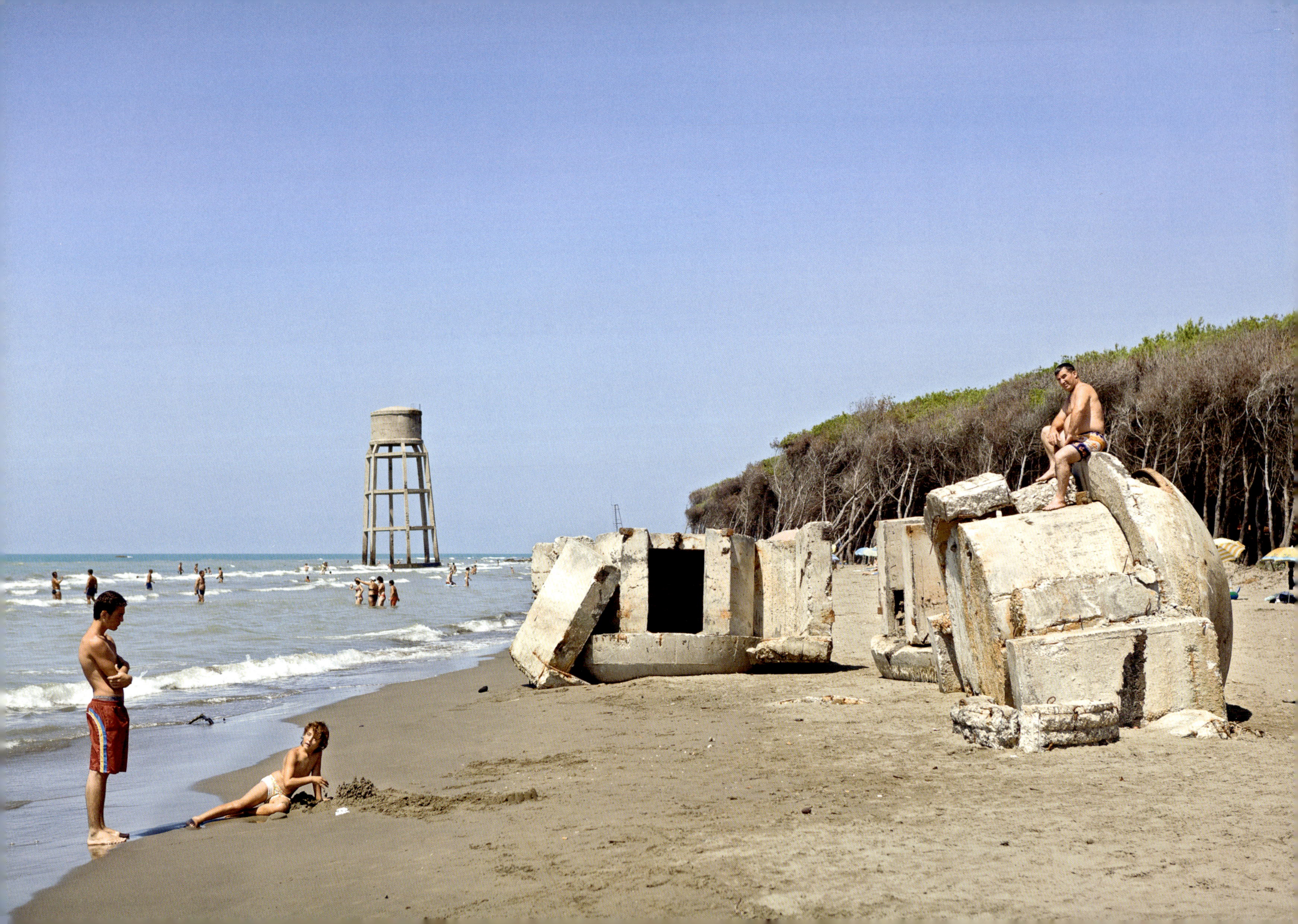

Robert Hackman

Metamorphosis

The Reuse of Albanian Bunkers from the Communist Era

introduced by

Genti Gjikola

DEWI LEWIS PUBLISHING

Wilting under an overexposed summer sun in 2001, I stood before a concrete monolith. In solitary abandon it dominated the street corner and was evidently unrelated to any of the neighbouring suburban houses. Unknown to me at the time, this structure would become an object of my focus for more than 10 years. As I approached this massive dome-shaped military construction I felt its power and authority, yet its unkept appearance indicated that its heyday was past: its threatening presence seemed almost malign. The weather had stained its hard exterior and weeds framed its solid base. I peered through the open aperture and waited for my eyes to adjust to the darkness within. Slowly a scene revealed itself to me and I was surprised to see that its interior was at odds with the brutish concrete outer shell. For here, within its dark belly, was a pool table. What initially felt threatening was in fact a social space for the community: a place of laughter and joviality, not solitude and isolation. Moments before I had been looking at a relic of the past and now I was scanning a scene of the present. The whole experience, like many Balkan experiences, was one of both confusion and the rushing excitement of discovery. I had entered Bunker Albania.

Over the following seven years I returned to Albania countless times undertaking various photographic assignments. My subjects were varied, yet one constant was omnipresent, the bunker. They filled every panorama and every turn, never shying from view. My initial introduction to this military architecture had stuck in my mind and I knew that one day I would begin to document their changing use and their juxtaposed outer and inner spaces. My work began in earnest in 2008.

Like many of us growing up in the West during the Cold War, the physical manifestations of this ‘conflict’ were like ghosts. Hidden from view behind the barbed wire fences of military bases, their destructive presence was felt but never seen. On rare occassions it was possible to see a permanent and mystifying structure from afar, or a fleeting aircraft, but never did this violence live amongst us, it lived only within us. As we look back on these haunted years we can easily question ourselves whether it really ever happened. Where is the evidence of this Cold War? Yet my wanderings through Albania left me with little doubt that there was once deep animosity between global ideologies. The bunkers made no effort to conceal themselves. They dominated the landscape, brutally unapologetic for the harsh doctrines from which they were born. Mass produced and devoid of any individuality, their sole purpose was to protect their communist masters and control the minds of the people who had to share their streets and lives with them.

These replicated concrete forms have not only been a connection between the past and present, but also a connection to the people of Albania I encountered whilst undertaking this project; their warmth and hospitality at odds with the objects I was photographing. Their individuality invades the dark inner spaces of these now defenceless bunkers, rewriting the turbulent history of their communist past with a spirit born not of ideology but of life, hope and a better tomorrow.

Robert Hackman

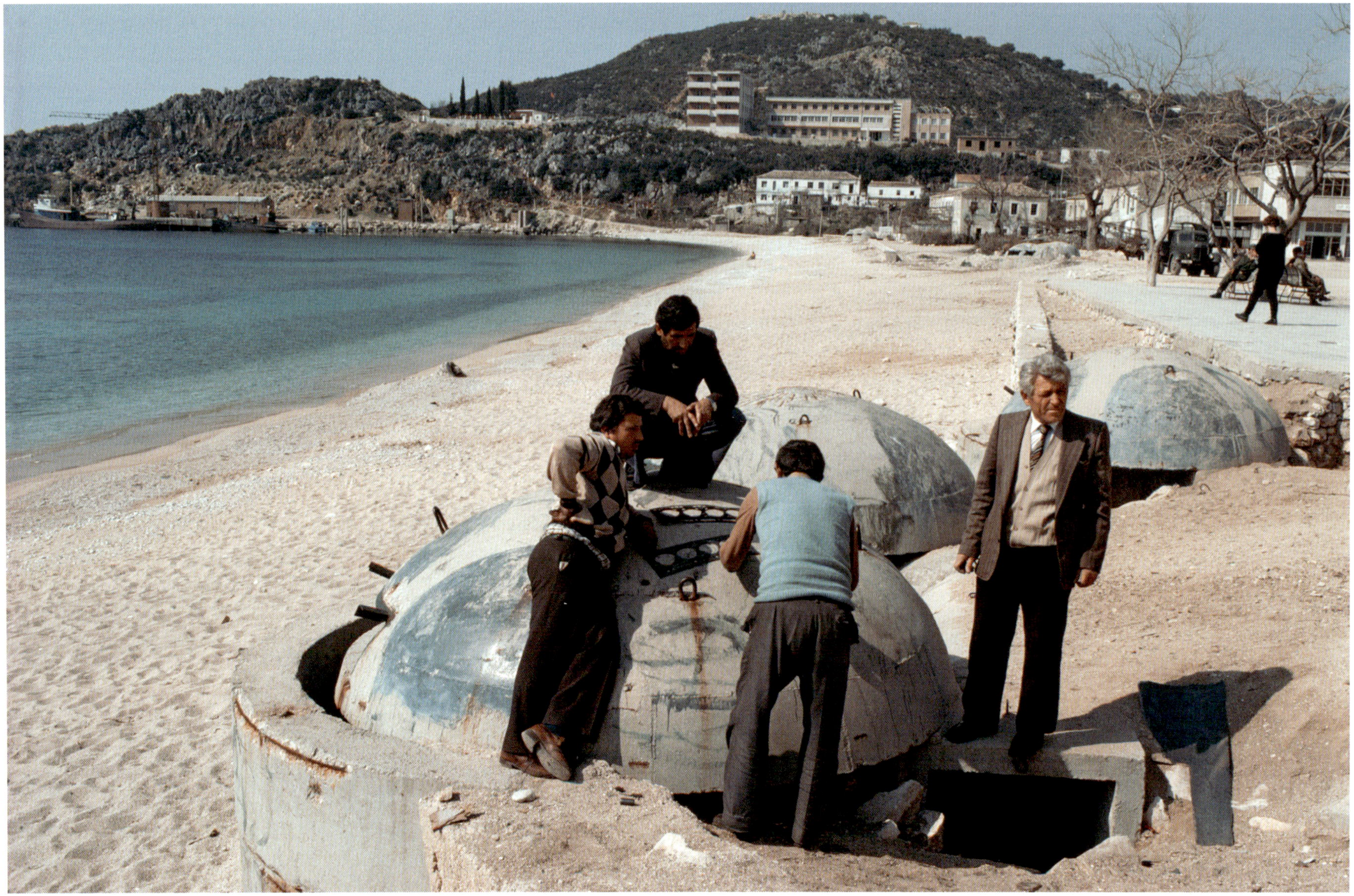

Martin Parr/MAGNUM PHOTOS, 1990

RECYCLING THE PAST

As I concentrated on these forms in the middle of apartment buildings, in courtyards, and on public squares, I felt as though a subterranean civilization had sprung up from the ground. This architecture's modern-ness was countered by its abandoned, decrepit appearance. These objects had been left behind, and were colorless; their grey cement relief was silent witness to a warlike climate.

Paul Virilio, *Bunker Archaeology*

Albania's idiosyncratic late 20th century history, especially the autarchic period between the late 1970s and 1990 when it had broken ties even with post Maoist–Deng Xiaopingist China and went it alone, has attracted a long line of defiant international photographers who saw the little Balkan country's existence and its ultra-left wing politics as a socialist paradise of sorts. Renowned names of European photography, from Michel Setboun through to Ferdinando Scianna, Josef Koudelka, Nikos Economopoulos, Martin Parr and many others, devised all sorts of ingenious and cunning plans just to gain entry and be able to capture the heart of this political and geographical enigma. Plans that involved cunning and meticulous attention to detail, through months, if not years (as in the case of Michel Setboun). To pierce the triple shield of iron fist/ concrete mushroom/barbed wire borders of the country, seemed almost as impossible as penetrating the sun.

The concrete mushrooms were the bunkers. Albania has attained a degree of notoriety throughout the world for its plethora of 20th century, communist-period military defence bunkers. Usually autocratic regimes, and even merely conservative ones, build walls, to keep those out, out, and those in, in, with the most famous of these structures being the Berlin Wall. But in Albania, as well as surrounding the closely guarded borders with all the barbed wire they could lay their hands on, the Marxist-Leninist rulers built numerous bunkers throughout the country. These served the double purpose of being a military fortification to prevent possible foreign invasion, and a tangible yet condescending, symbolic presence of the might of Enver Hoxha, the country's severe leftist leader. He was omnipresent and the bunkers were his disquieting sentries; an eerie, chilling reminder of the nation's domineering father figure to its nearly three million people. Enver Hoxha's vision and the all-pervading paranoia that characterized the last two decades of his life (from 1961 to his death in 1985 he never set foot outside Albania), have yet to be fully dissected and comprehended.

The bunkers were a massive project intended to instil a sense of rupture in the strictly controlled metronome of Albanian daily life. The golden age of Albanian bunker building (roughly 1974 to 1988) introduced to the national diet of ever-diminishing food supplies, the terror of upcoming, imminent war. Yet the purpose of the bunkers was not the outright protection of the fatherland and its communist ideals from capitalist or imperialist invaders, although this was said to be the sole reason they were built. No. The primary goal of the bunkers was the protection of Hoxha's own idiosyncratic fiefdom of purges and terror. They formed an anxious, last-man-standing plan to protect the rest of his family, and the precious few political comrades-in-arms, who, after years of systematic

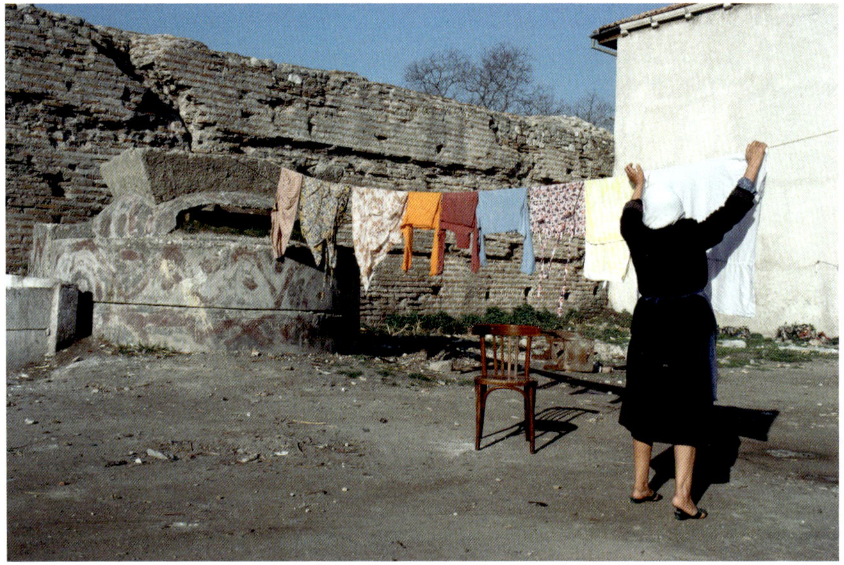

Martin Parr/MAGNUM PHOTOS, 1990

purges, were left to ceaselessly venerate the legacy of Hoxha's reign. The bunkers sought to protect this blood-drenched status quo, long after Hoxha had died. These acolytes strived to control Albania, even after his death, in the same spirit as he had done, through a specific conditioning of the Albanian mind: always fearful and ready for war, no longer capable of independent thought, forever waiting for the 'enemy'. An image that the State ceaselessly conjured up in order to affirm its existence. Bunkers were not aimed at the enemy. Bunkers were aimed at the sands of time.

* * *

How many bunkers were built is still a matter of debate, ranging from the lowest estimate of 150,000 to an improbable 750,000. I believe it to be somewhere between 167,000 and 175,000, for the simple reason that this is the figure often quoted in interviews or on TV programmes by the military personnel and officials involved in the construction process. These experts repeatedly mention detailed maps of every bunker ever constructed, but such maps still cannot be disclosed due to state and military secrecy. For this reason, wild claims about their number topping three quarters of a million abound.

The bunkers were home-made, made-in-Albania, both in terms of design and production, if for no other reason that their structure could not be disclosed to any 'enemy state' after Albania summarily cut itself off from any superpower support or aid. Legend has it that the Albanian engineer responsible for their design was so certain the bunkers would be able to withstand an enemy attack that, before production started on a national scale, he asked for a bunker to be tested against heavy artillery fire, including rockets, with him inside, alone, manning the pill-box. Both engineer and bunker passed this test and mass production began in earnest. This is why the architecture of the bunker form overpowers local topography, achieving an undisputed monopoly of form and function over landscape and nature. Military primacy overruled the rhythm of daily life and the brutalist silhouette of these concrete half-spheres was the true horizon where the sun's last rays sank daily.

In the late 1980s, when the Eastern European winds of change finally breezed through Albania, bunker production came to a halt. In the end, Albania's enormous concrete legacy reputedly left the country with more bunkers than houses, more bunkers than soldiers, and definitely more bunkers than cars (in 1985 Albania had only 1,265). During the communist era, foreign photographers were closely monitored and strictly forbidden from taking pictures of the defence bunkers. Turkish photographer Mehmet Biber paid a visit in 1980 and was stunned by their sheer, overwhelming number. He did not capture any bunkers with his camera and even his attempt to replicate images from postcards was blocked by his guide. Yet sometimes in the middle of the dictatorship, it was still possible to record one of the hundreds of thousands of the fortifications. In several truly memorable images, French photographer Michel Setboun shows us how these oversize bunkers looked at the time of construction (both photos dated mid-1980s), providing evidence of these edifices before they were eventually abandoned. In early 1990, the British photographer Martin Parr also captured the bunkers in the final months before the collapse of the one-party state, flowering again and again, even in the most unexpected places.

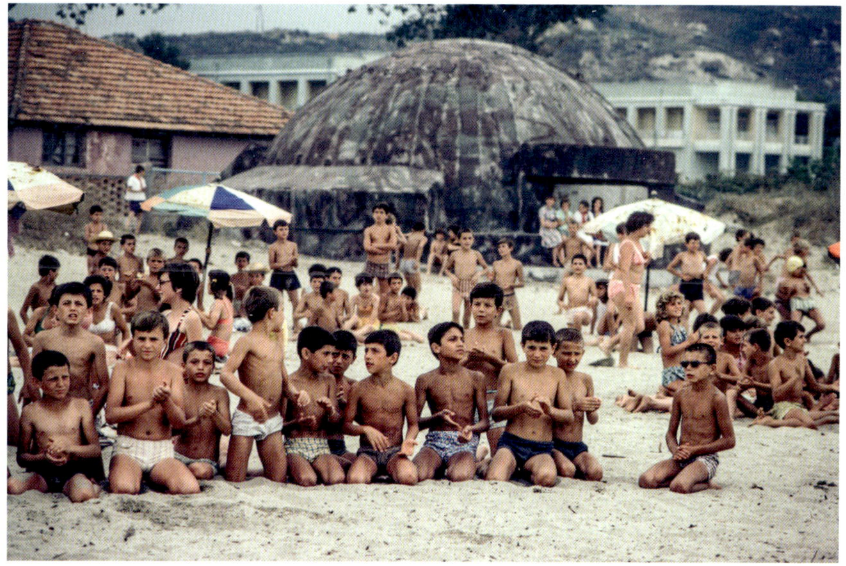

Michel Setboun, 1984

...what branches grow, out of this stony rubbish?
T. S. Eliot, *The Wasteland*

Robert Hackman has photographed these bunkers from a point in time, two decades on, when these objects no longer make sense, as if from the military chrysalis a contemporary piece of art has evolved. It seems to me that Hackman's fascination with the bunkers stems from their ubiquity as a site of psychological anguish. In many photographs there is a tangible sense of loss, a purposeless existence with the primitive and charged atmosphere in so many of the compositions reminding one of an early surrealist Dali painting, of Cavafy's poem *Waiting for the Barbarians*, or Dino Buzzati's superb Kafkaesque novel *The Tartar Steppe*. Hackman has captured Albania's resilient bunkers at a stage in their lives when they seem docile and unthreatening, senile and bizarre, inviting and repellent. From these photographs these derelict pill-boxes proclaim their particular powerlessness in a supposed time of 'peace'. These Cold War relics scream their solitude in times of globalised conflict, deprived from the fertile environment of the grand, clashing ideologies of the 20th century. Hackman offers Hoxha's bunkers with their military vehemence transformed into functional impotence, an intransigence of use that ultimately was never utilised. The deep savagery of war between Hoxha's soldiers welded inside bunkers versus the promised foreign invaders never took place: the brutal shelling, the catharsis of combat, the glorious battles, the paroxysm of agitation, planes flying ominously over the dramatic landscape, fortifications built with tremendous sacrifice by a

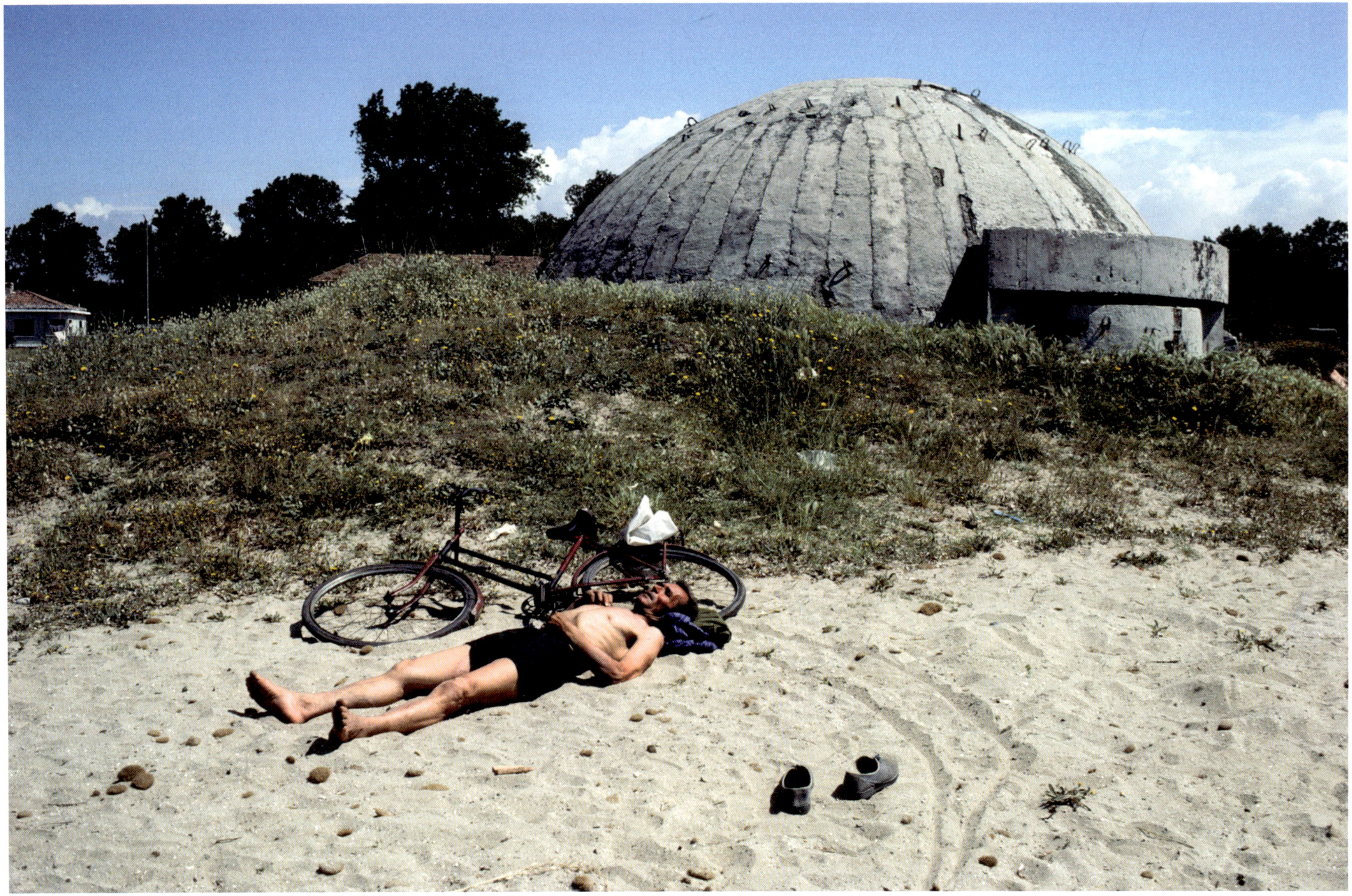

Michel Setboun, 1984

desperate rearguard holding the line, worthy of historical memoirs or heroic screenplays, would be forever unknown to them.

Hackman's odyssey, covering almost every corner of the country, records his search to understand the phenomenon of Albania's bunkerisation and their baffling transformation in the post-socialist reality. Save for those few still being used by the Albanian army (cue the irony: a NATO member since 2009), the overwhelming majority of the remaining bunkers are now totally abandoned. As Hackman has shown in various photographs, the bunkers presently resemble land art that won't be disappearing any time soon, despite vigorous attempts to uproot the structures and remove the usable iron and concrete slabs for civilian construction. Those durable bunkers, that stand in the way of the entrepreneurial local spirit of wild west capitalism that overwhelmed the nation in the wake of Albania's extreme brand of Marxism-Leninism, have been transformed (if a bunker can ever be transformed) and re-used as bachelor pads, homeless shelters, family houses, bars, restaurants, public toilets, pigsties, barns, small manufacturing workshops, ammunition depots, canteens, watchtowers, security guard huts, water depots and lime cisterns, Christian churches or alternative places of worship, waste containers, hotels, museums, and occasionally a meeting point for furtive sexual encounters (even back in the days of Enver Hoxha, this transgressive pleasure was quite in vogue).

Hackman shows us how these strange architectural bodies, like objects hardened in some hellish furnace, have undergone nearly three decades worth of unbelievable camouflage and mimetism. Hackman's compelling visual report is photographically matter-of-fact. It introduces the viewer to the peculiarities of the phenomenon and oscillations of space and geography while keeping a safe distance from the continual political and historical turmoil of this small Balkan country. His is not a study of bunker typologies during the turbulent Cold War years but a search for how resourcefully people adapt to surreal circumstances, how history is shaped even by victims or serendipitous 'victors'.

The dynamic colours and the blue skies that pop out of these repurposed military constructions highlight the incongruence of finding these structures located in a Mediterranean climate. Hackman captures the layers of the oxidative patina and the pick-and-mix makeovers; work carried out by ordinary people triumphs, de-stressing everyday 'capitalist heroism' and hinting at the lack of state control, or safety and building codes in these times of open borders. A fitting comparison would be that Robert Hackman looks at Albania's bunkers as if from a notable distance, like the relief of the earth as seen by the astronauts.

Beyond the limits of his specific subject matter and the bunkers' rustic existence another sphere of human interaction begins. Let's not forget: deep inside the concrete heart of these structures, one could hardly ever see how truly big the sky was.

Genti Gjikola

Genti Gjikola studied Geography and History at Tirana State University; Architecture of Interiors (Hons) at Oxford Brookes University, UK, and holds an MA from Bartlett School of Architecture, University College London, in Architectural History. From 2008 to April 2018 he was the Head of the Exhibitions Department at the Albanian National Gallery of Arts in Tirana. In April 2018 he became curator for the Centre for Openness and Dialogue (COD), a unique art-and-culture space at the Office of the Prime Minister of Albania. Genti Gjikola's artworks were included in the 52nd Venice Biennale in 2007 as part of the Albanian Pavilion.

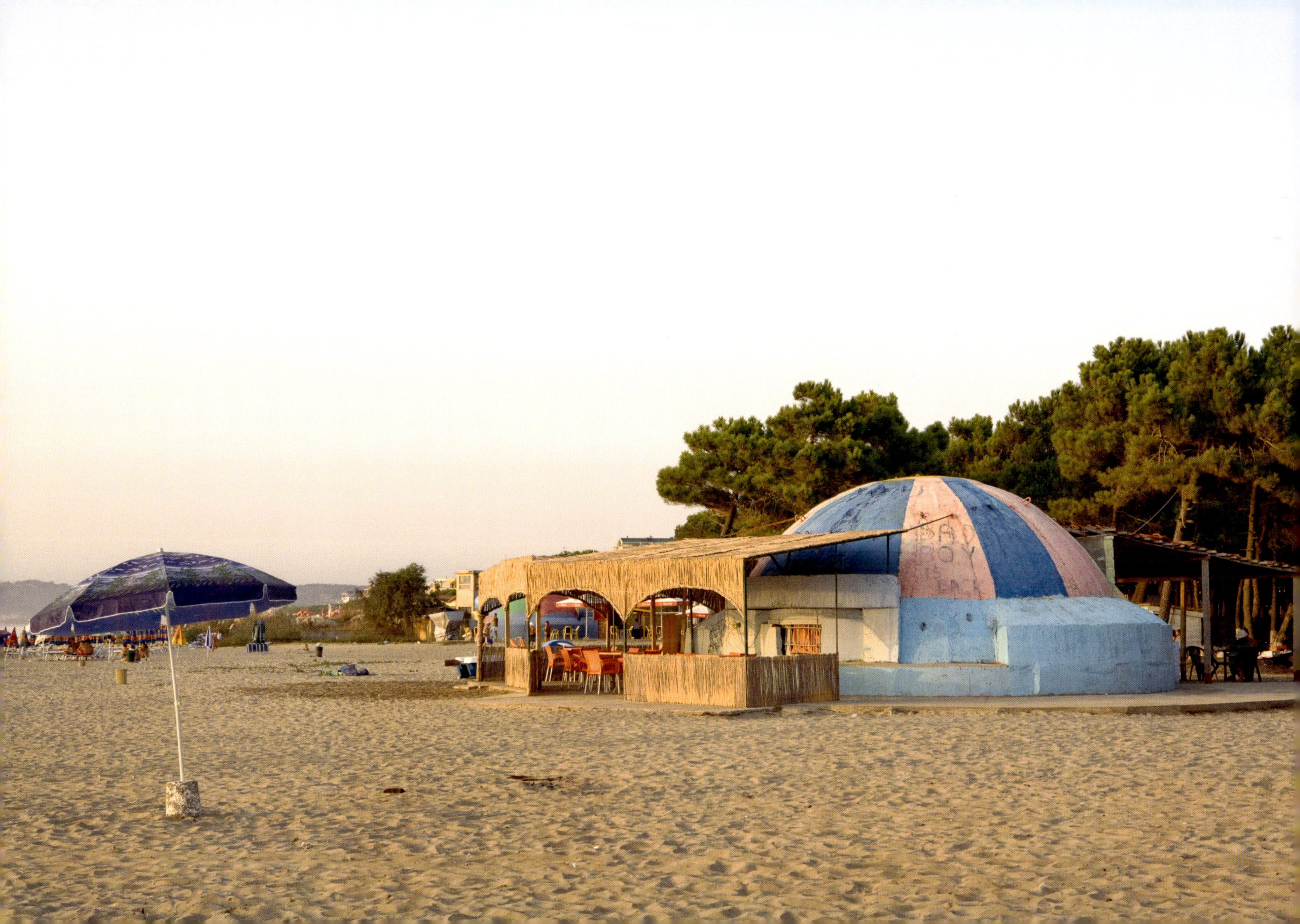

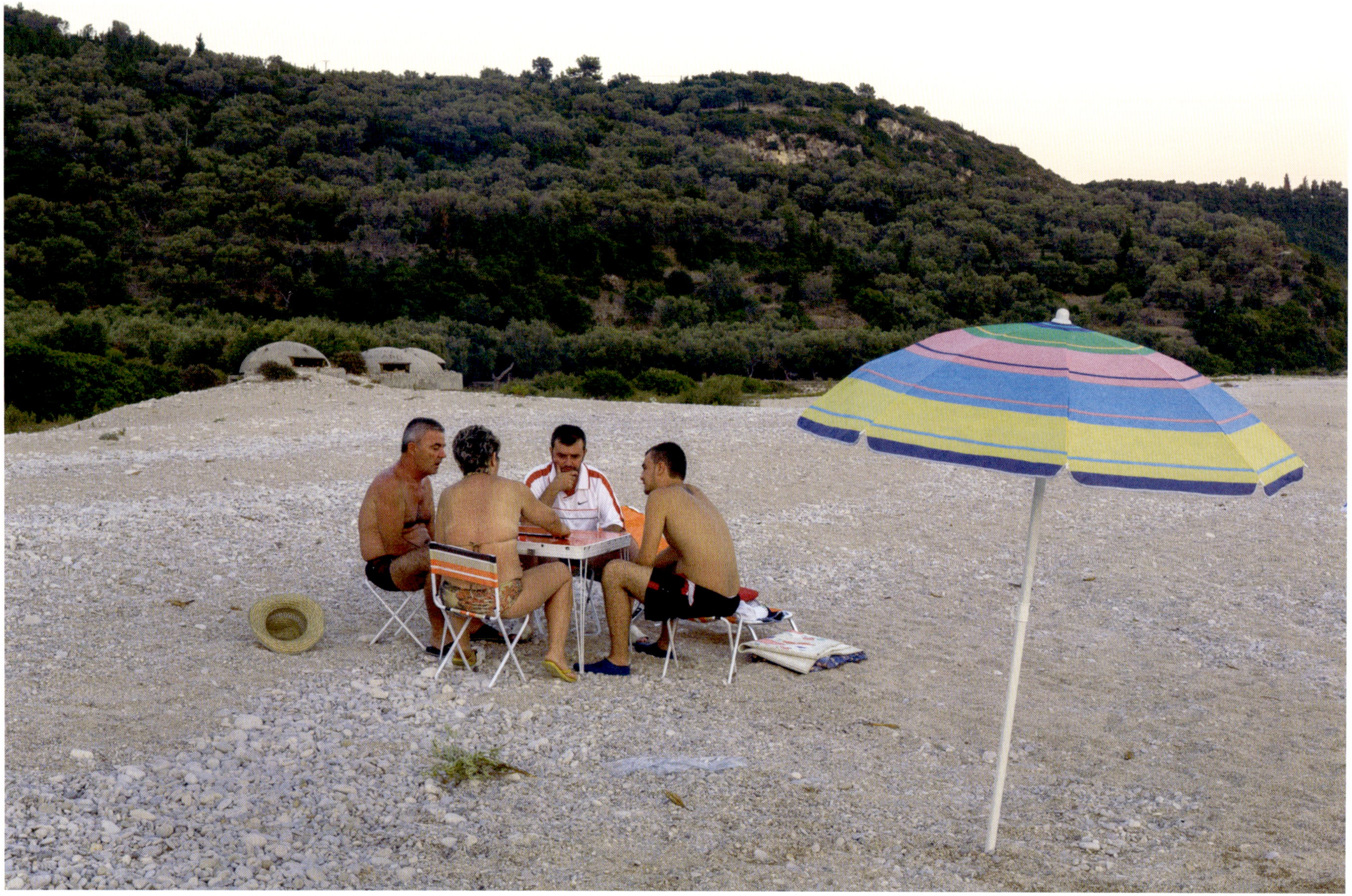

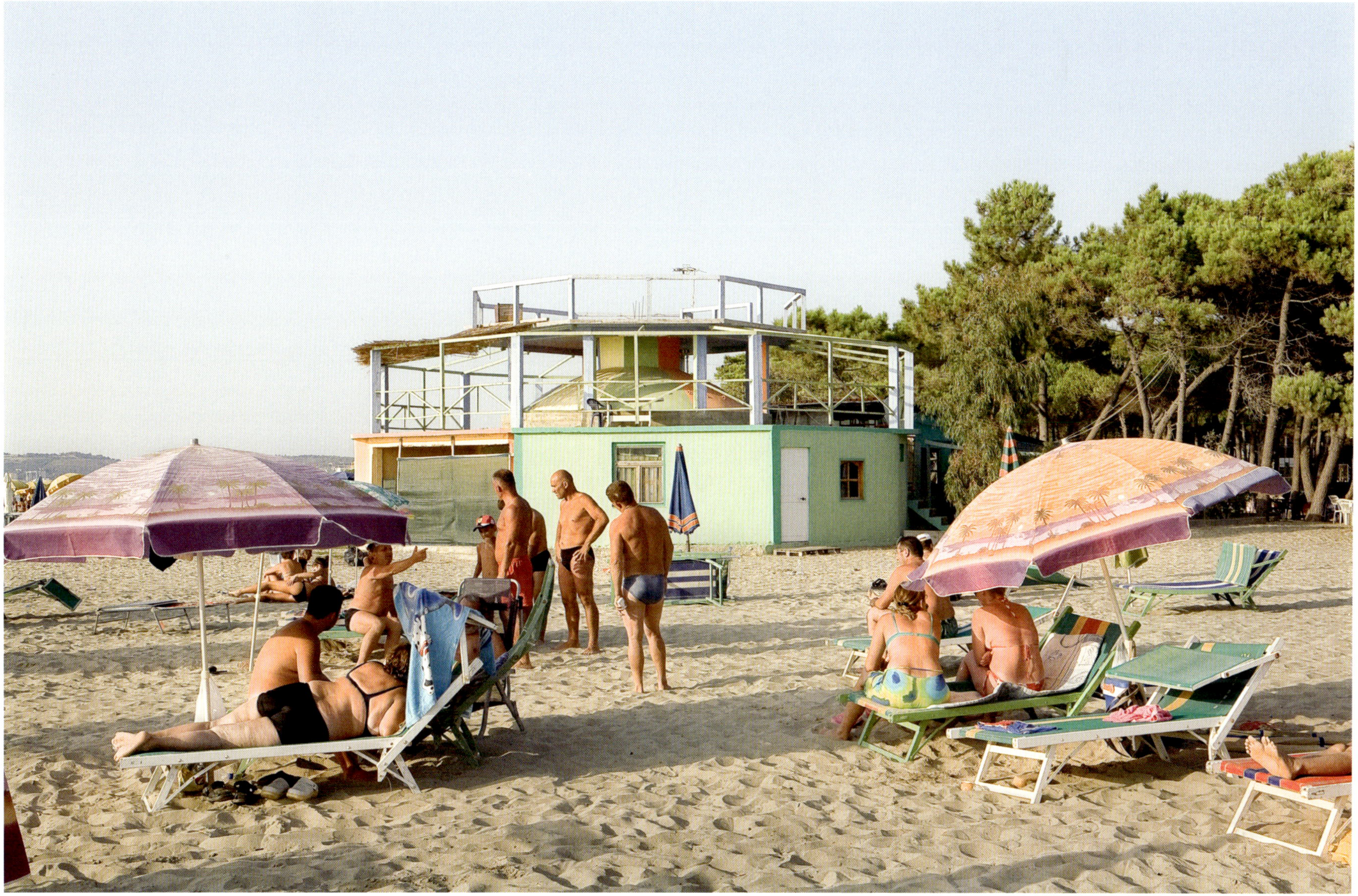

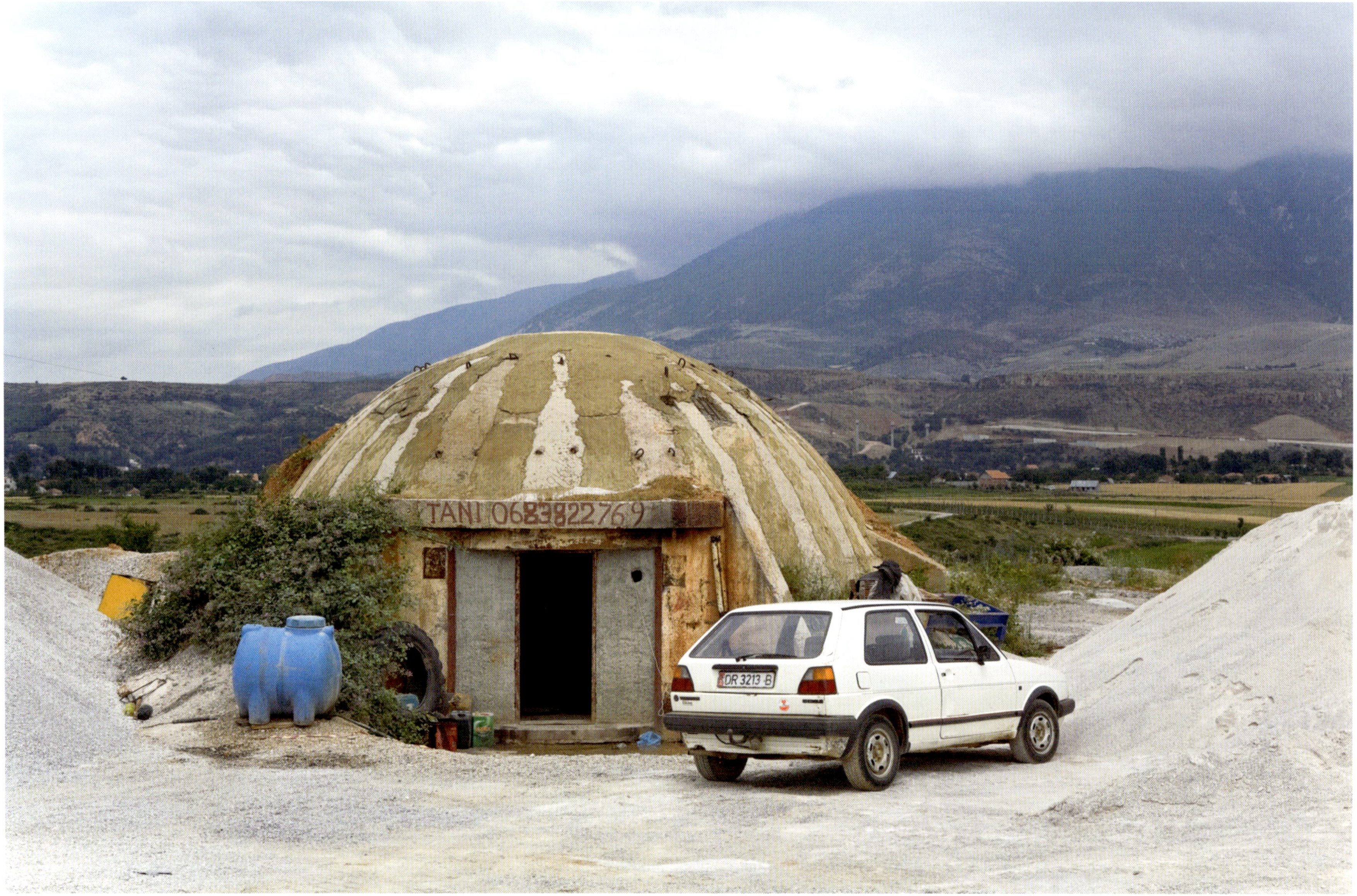
TANI
DR 3213 B

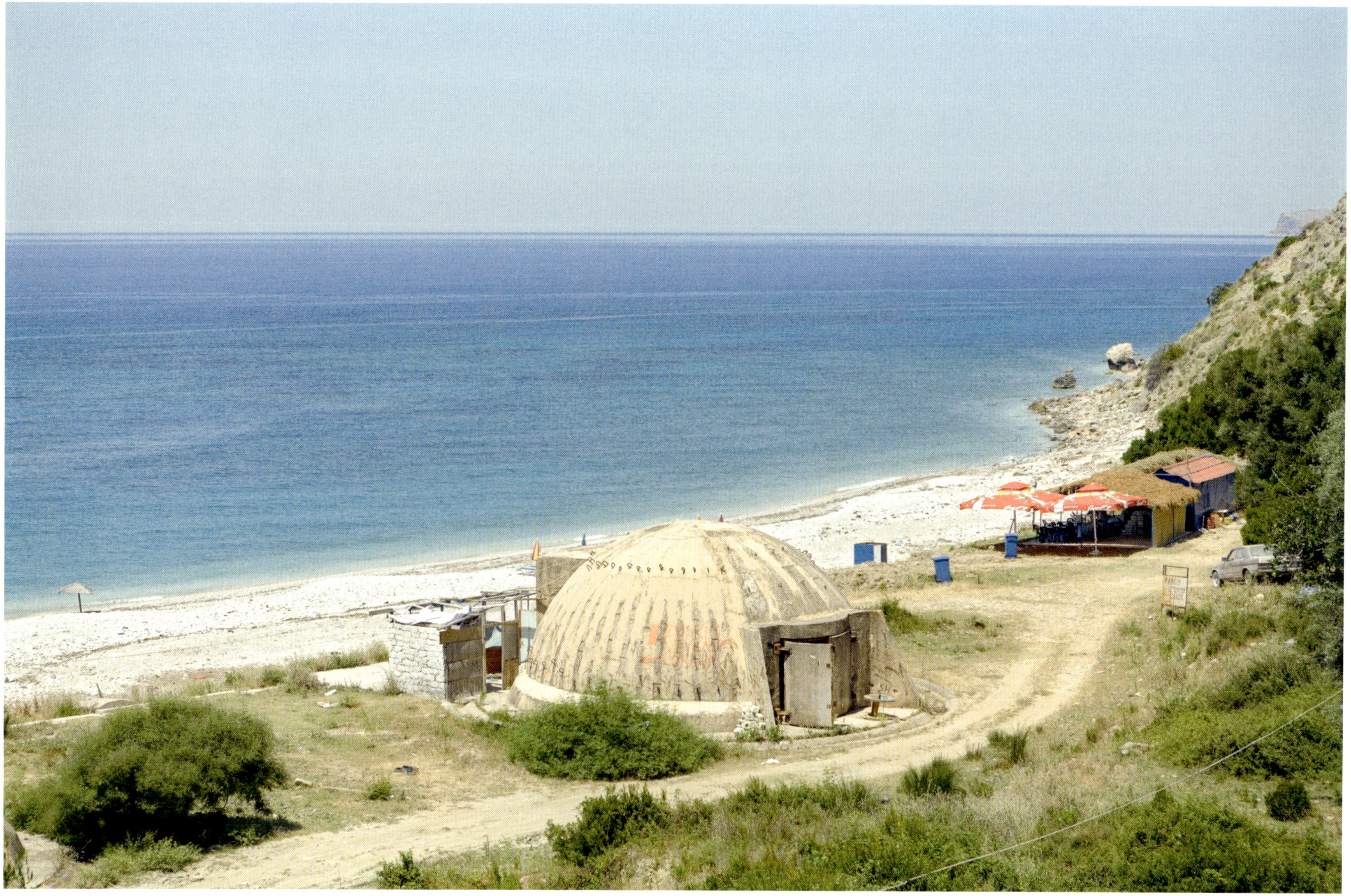

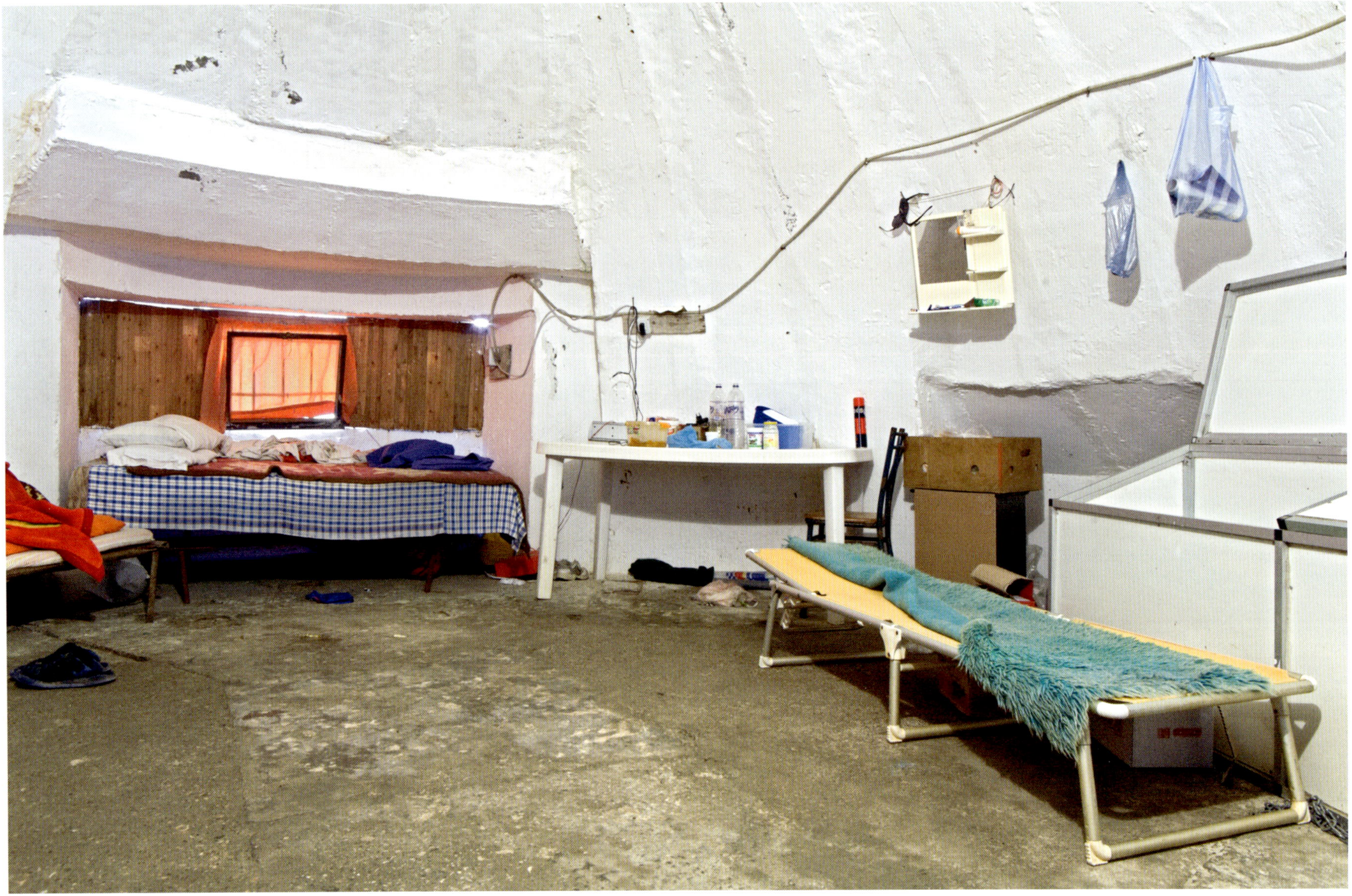

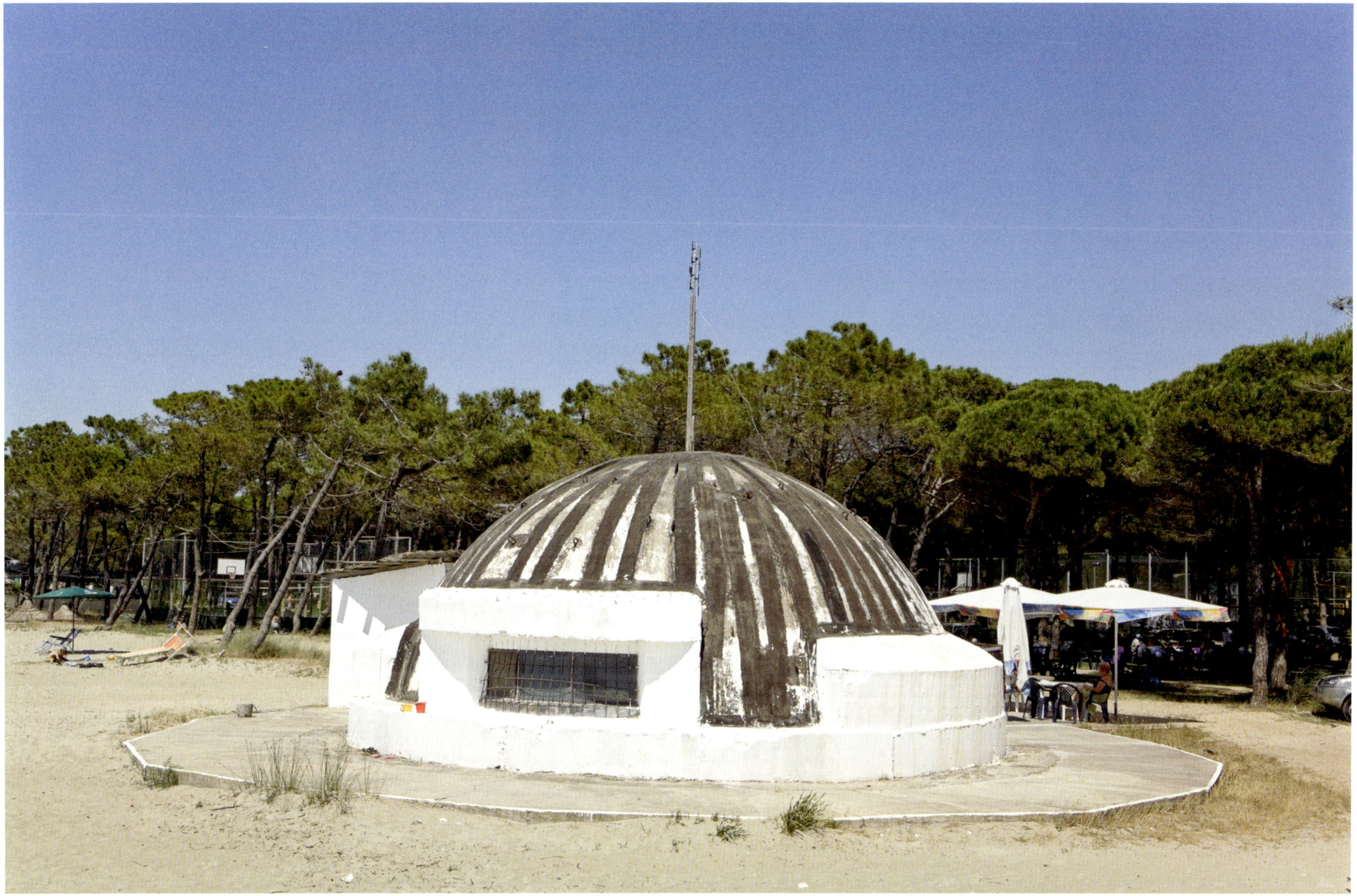

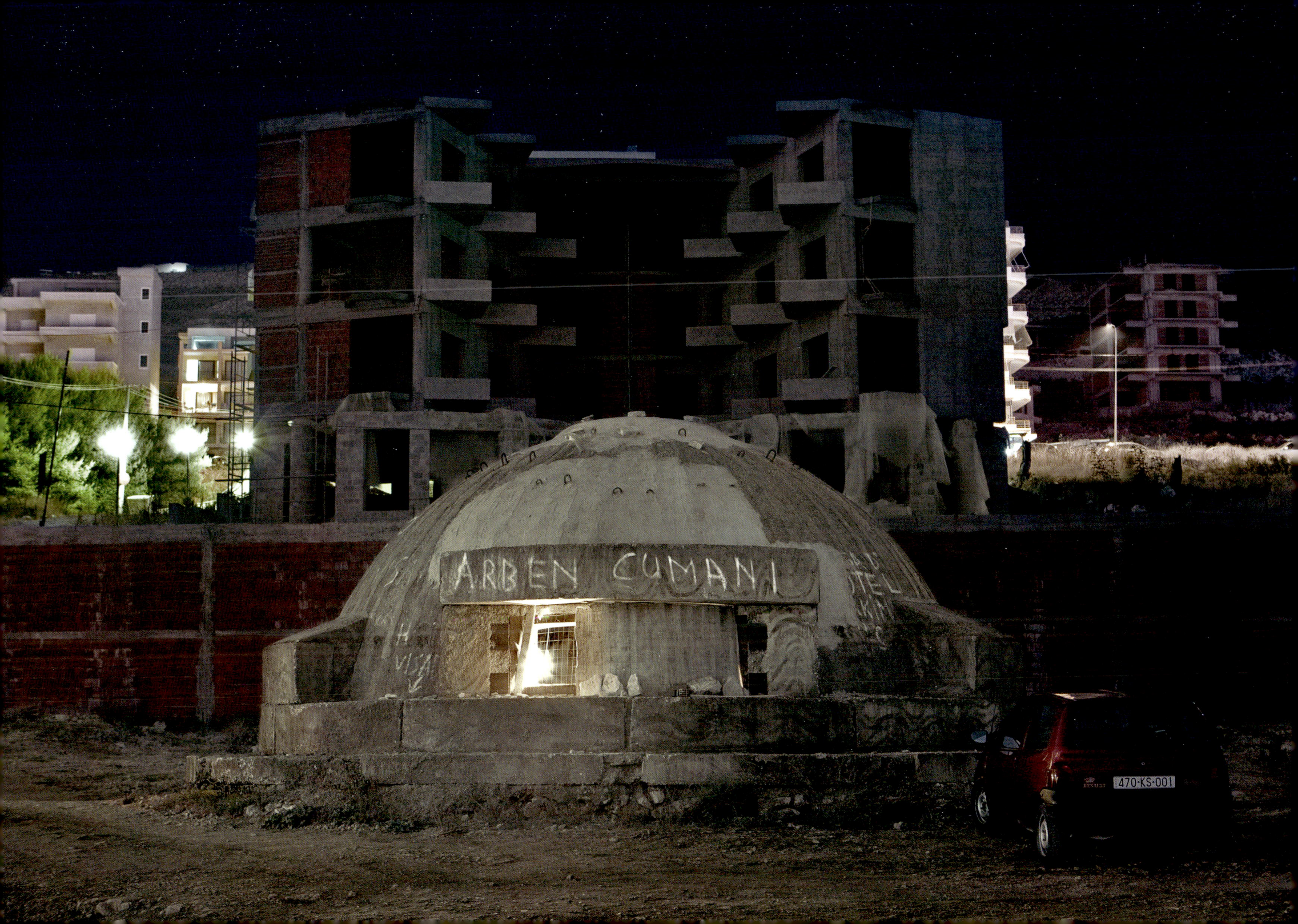
ARBEN CUMANI
470-KS-001

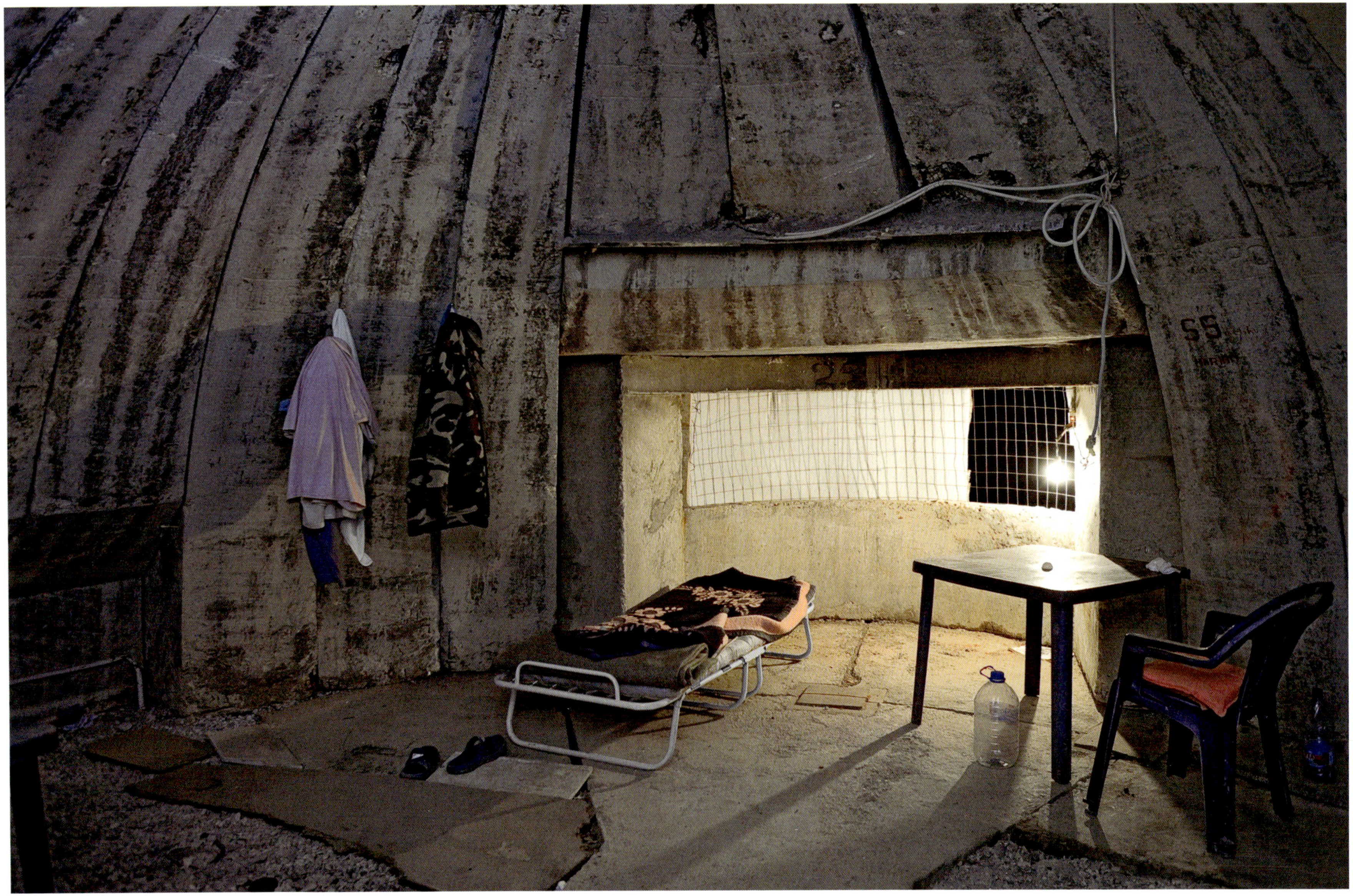

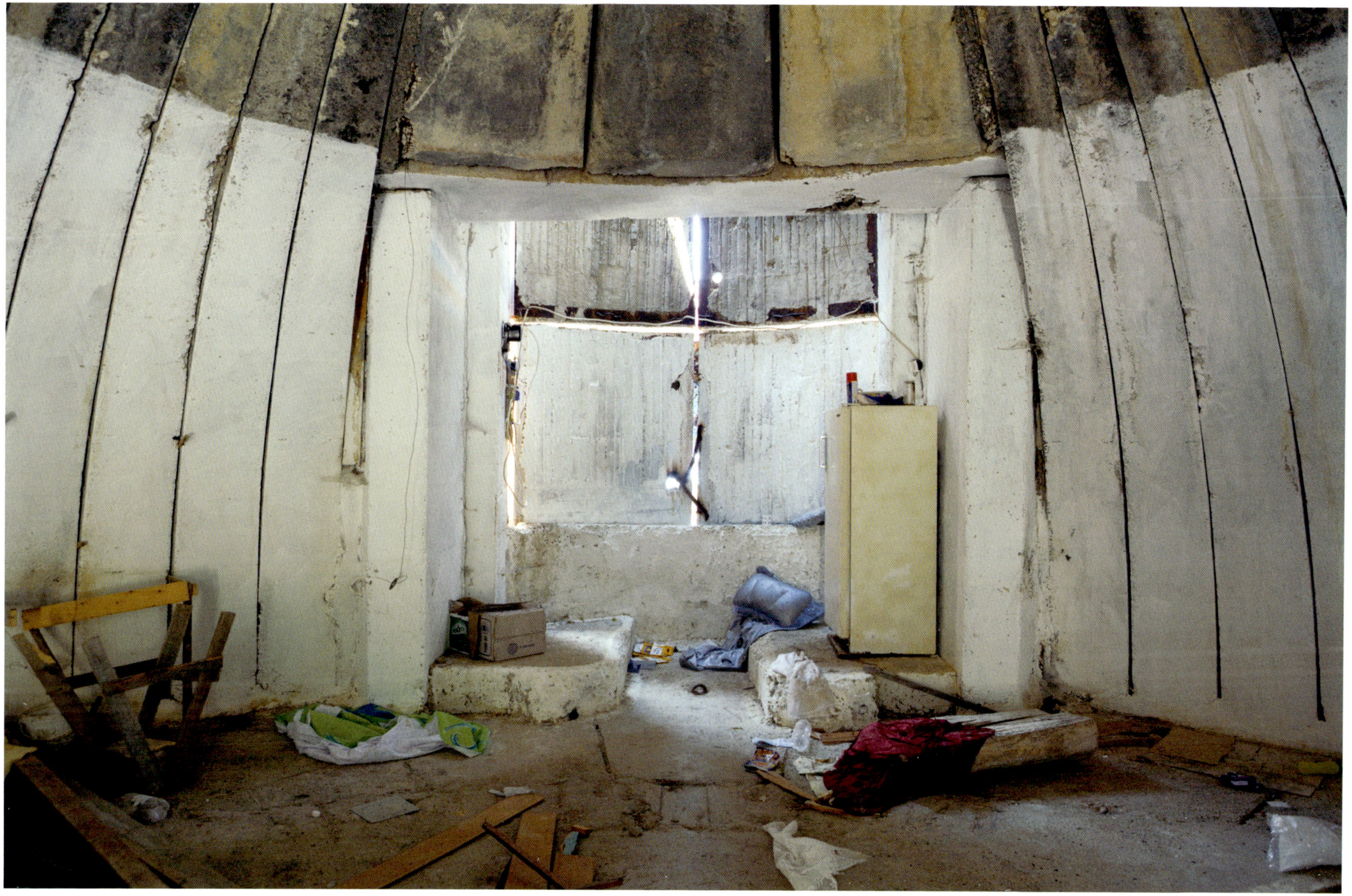

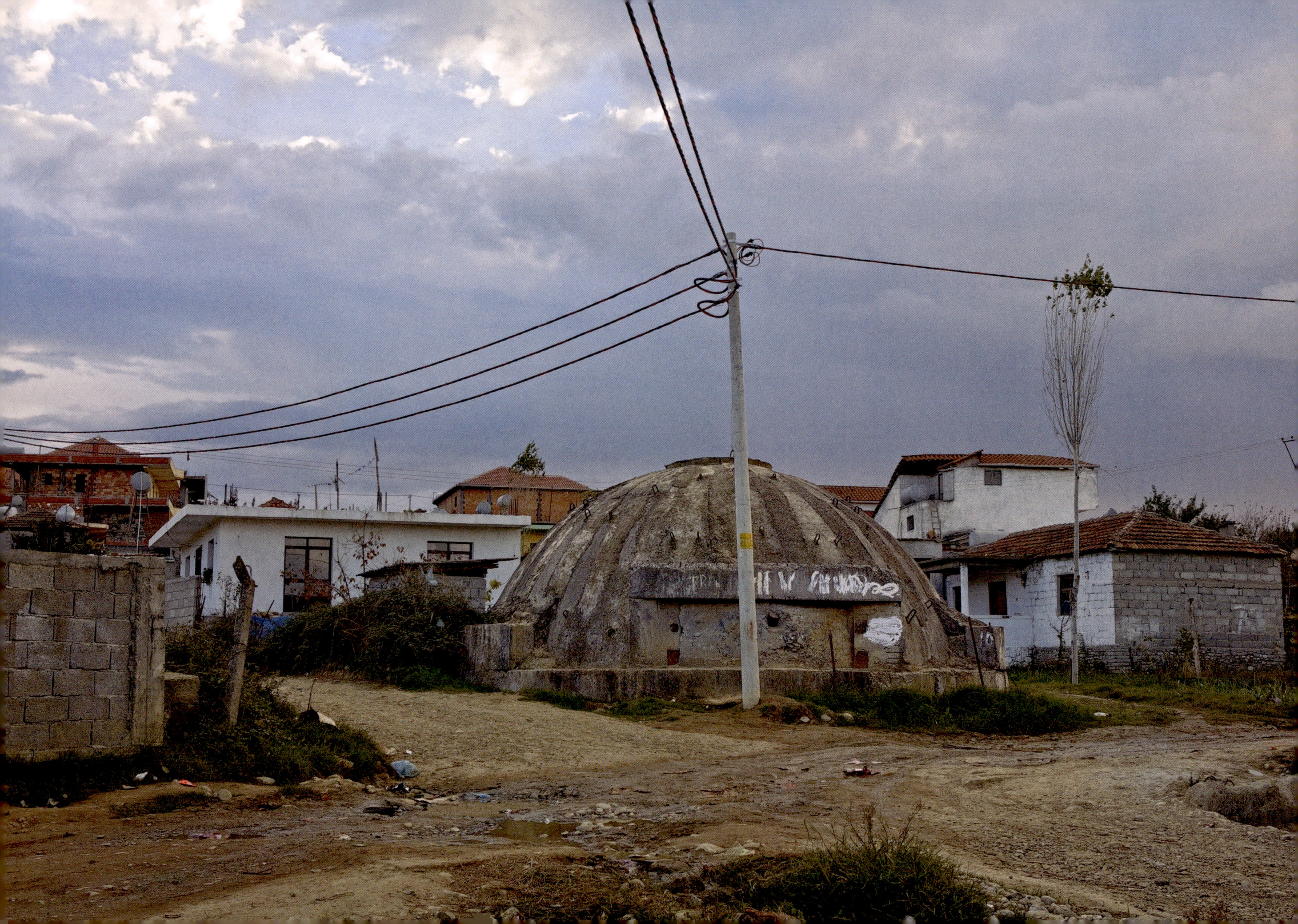

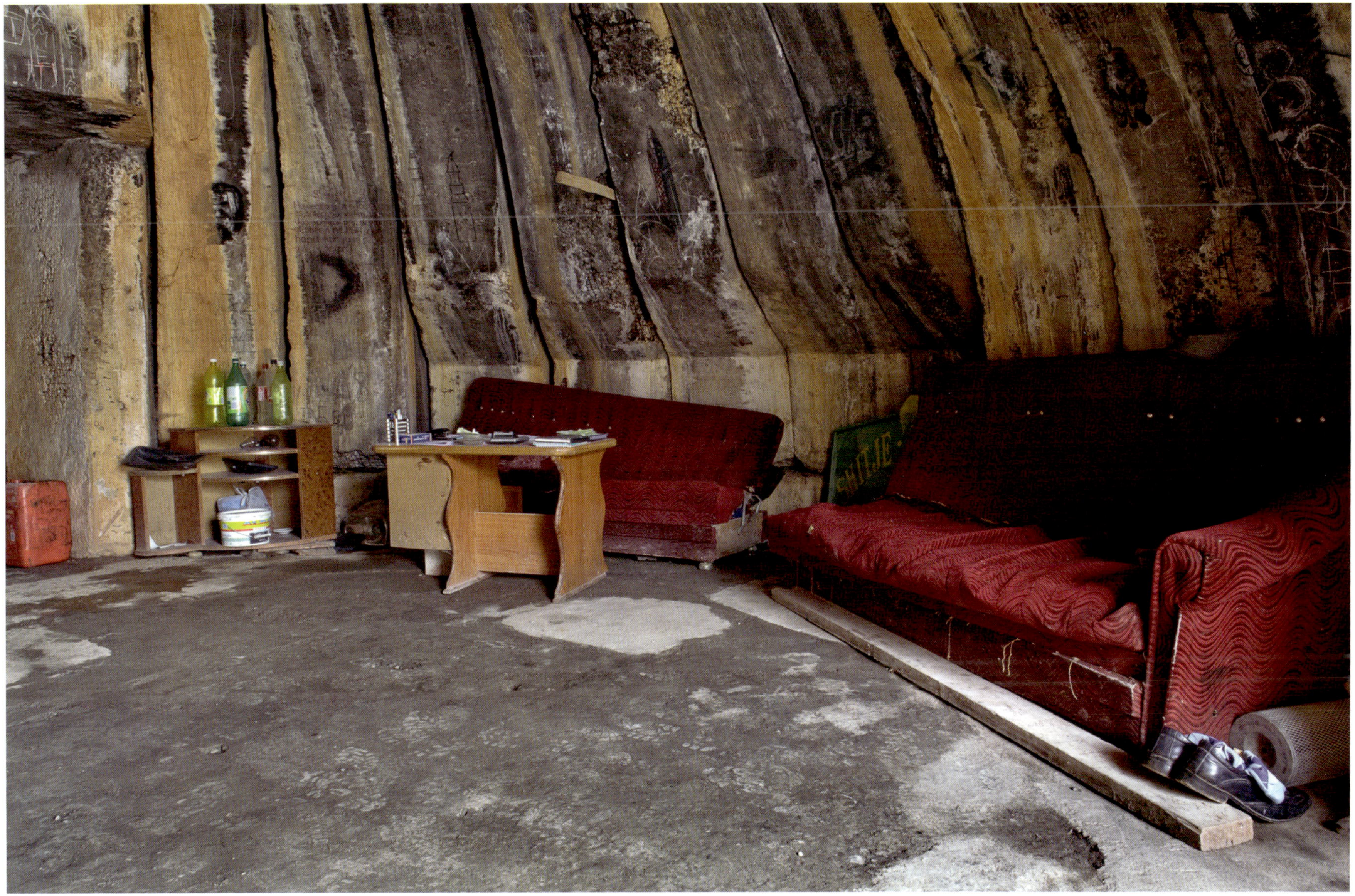

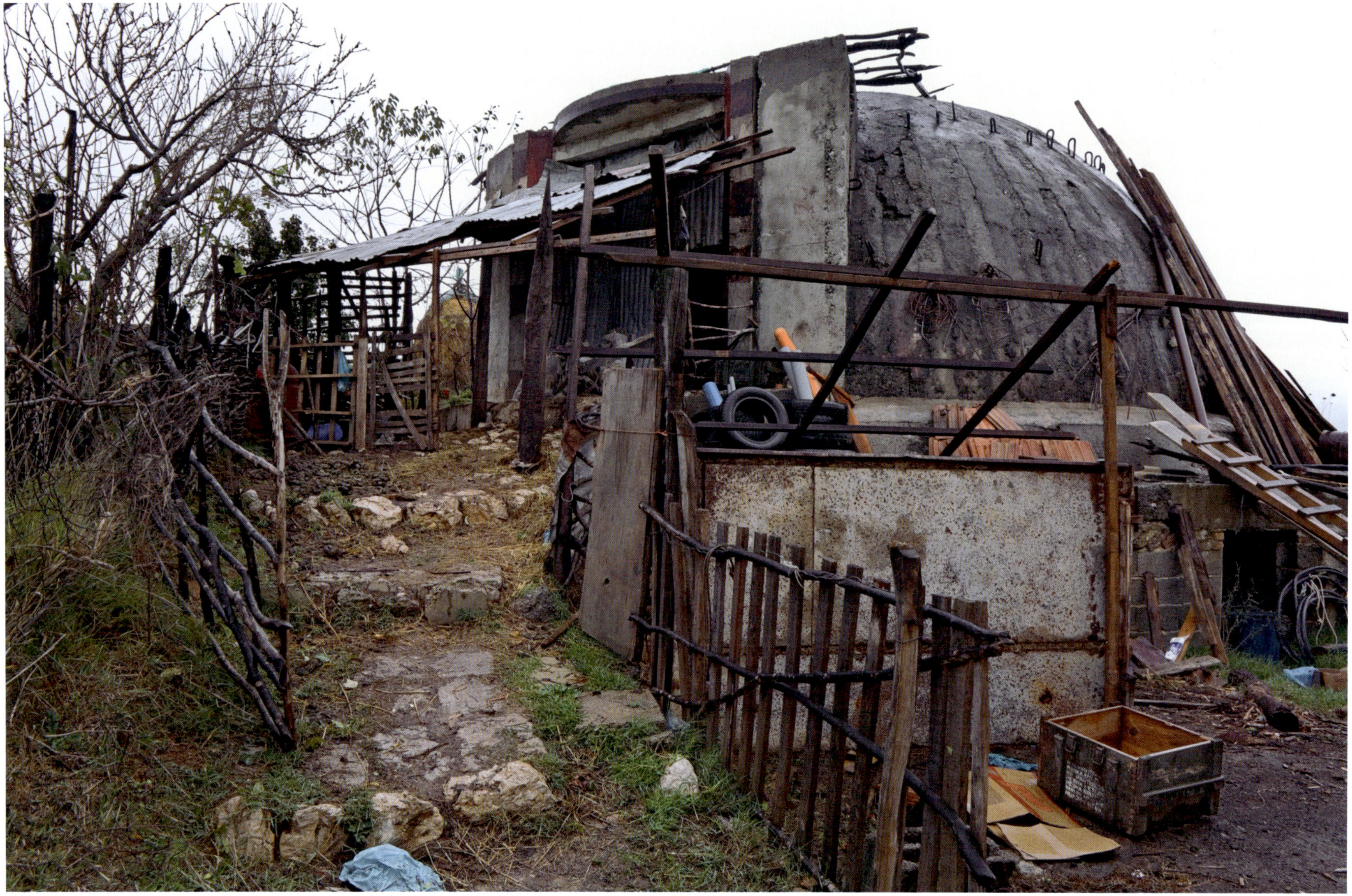

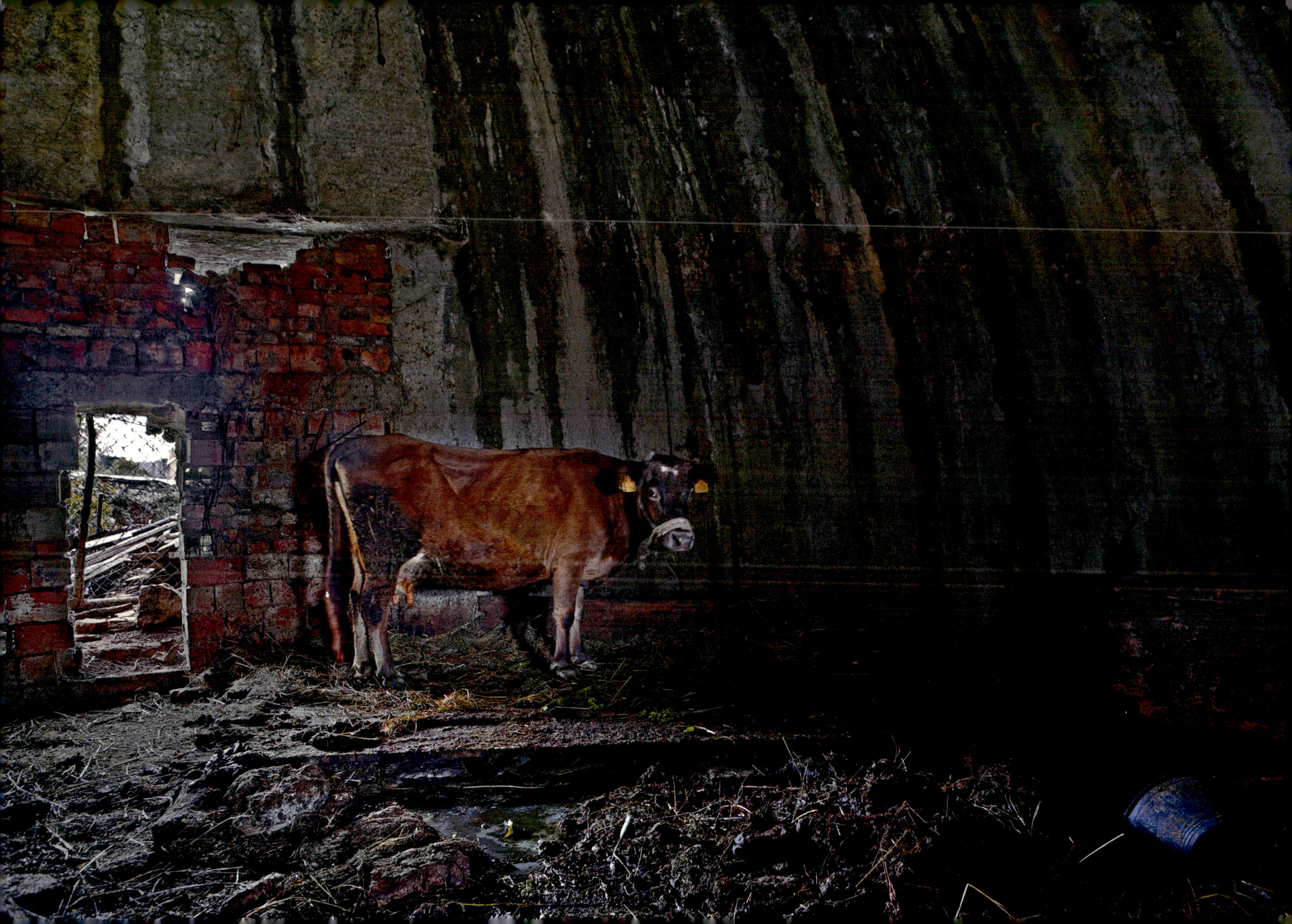

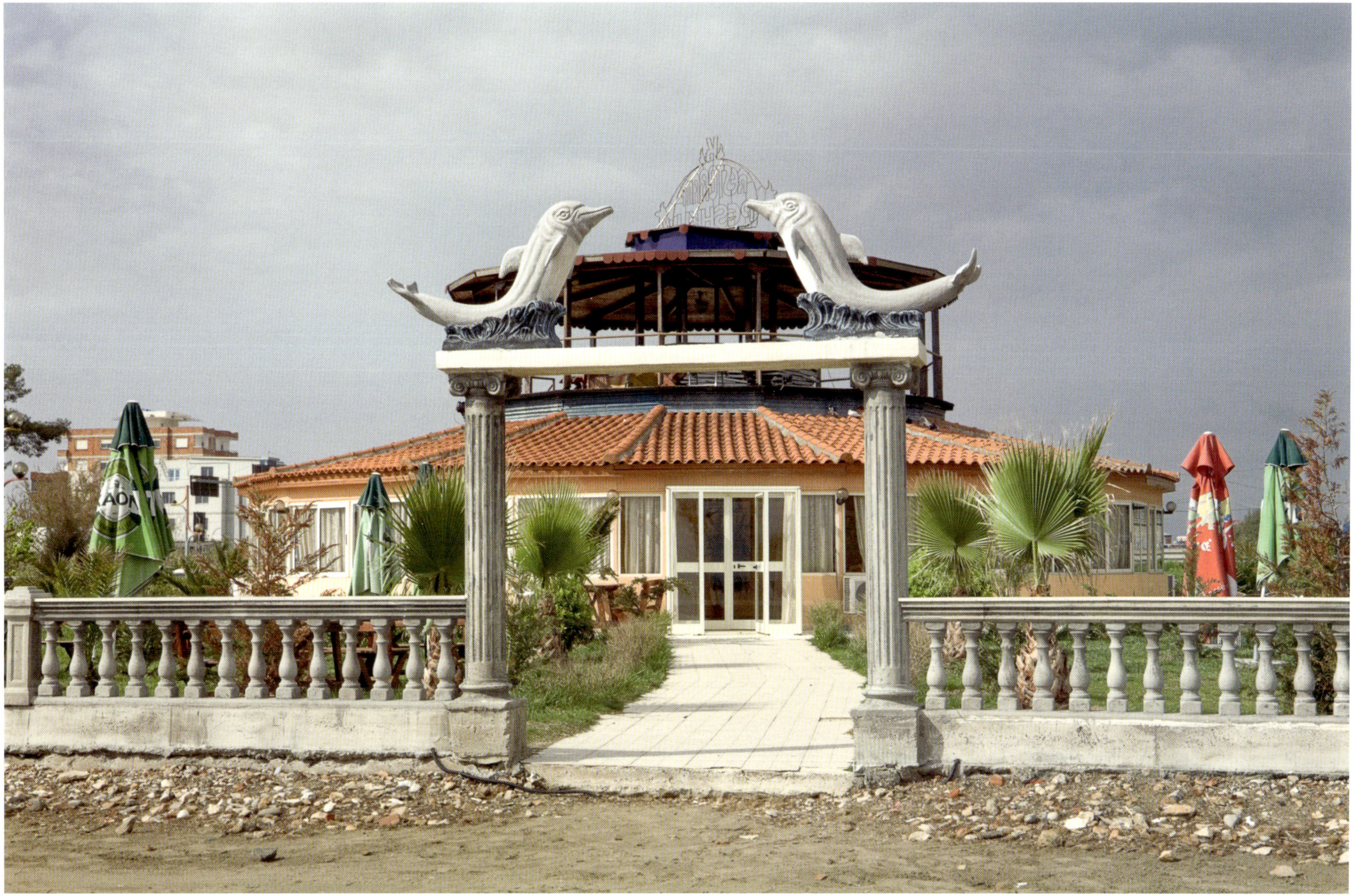

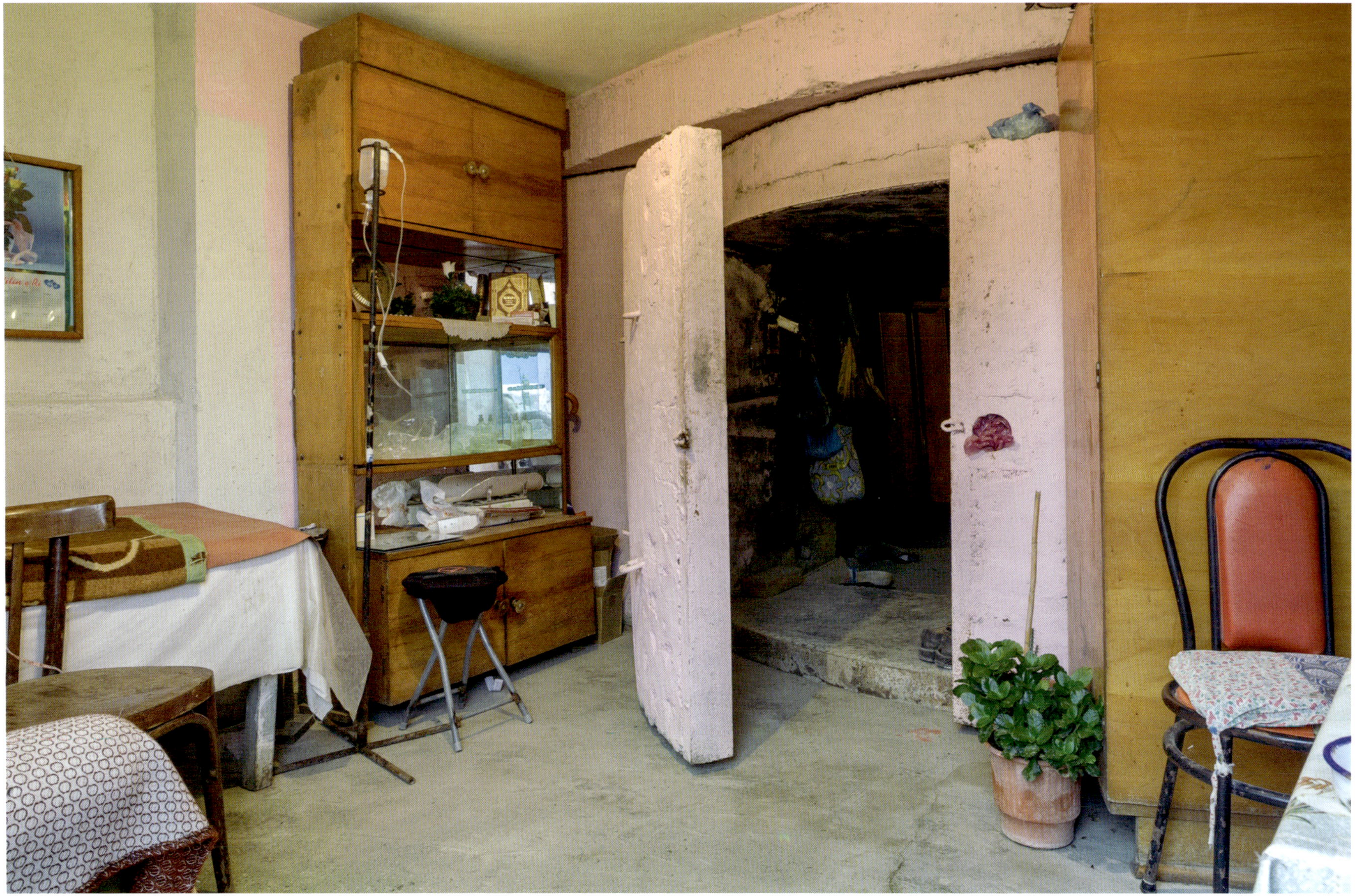

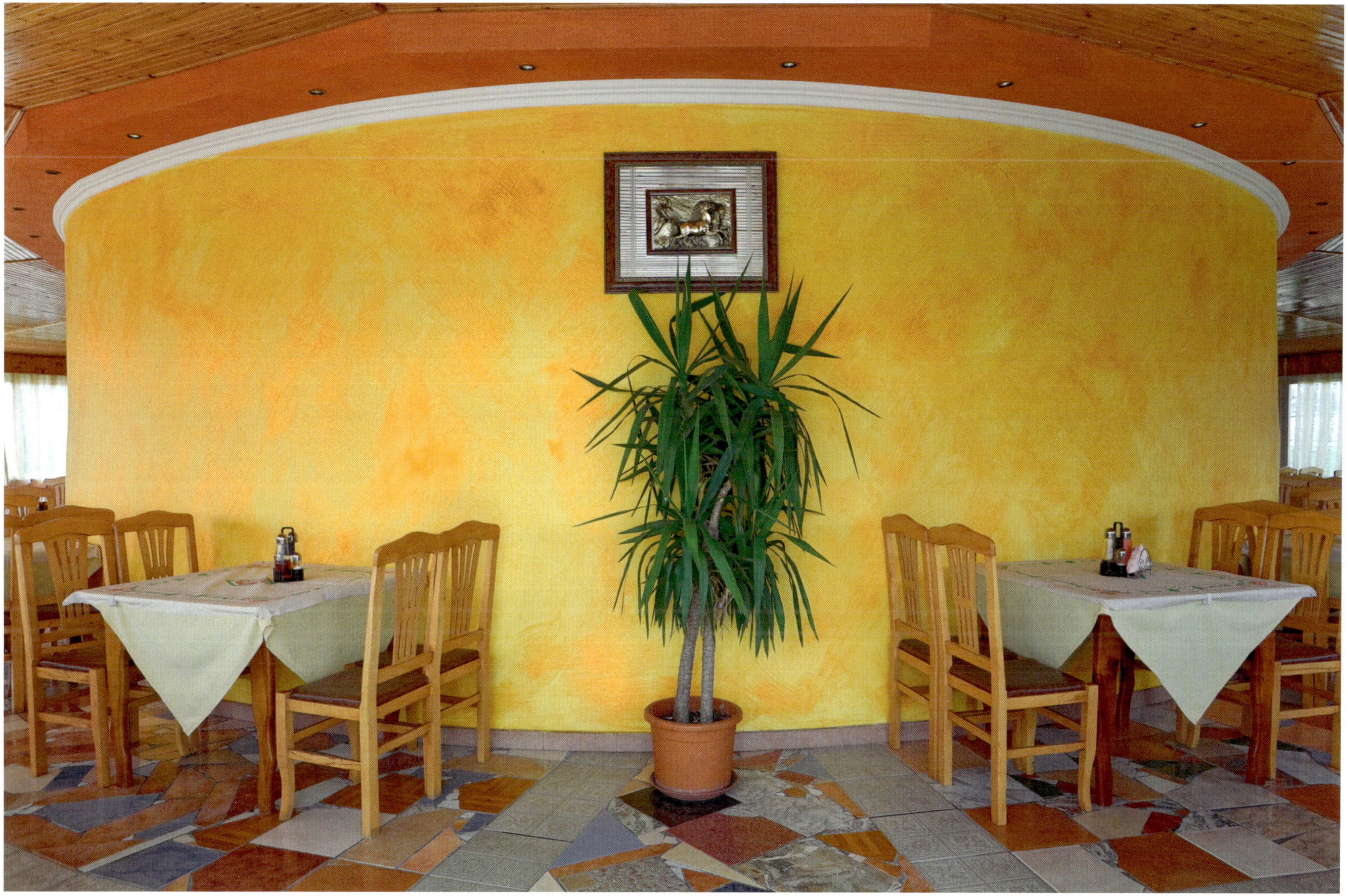

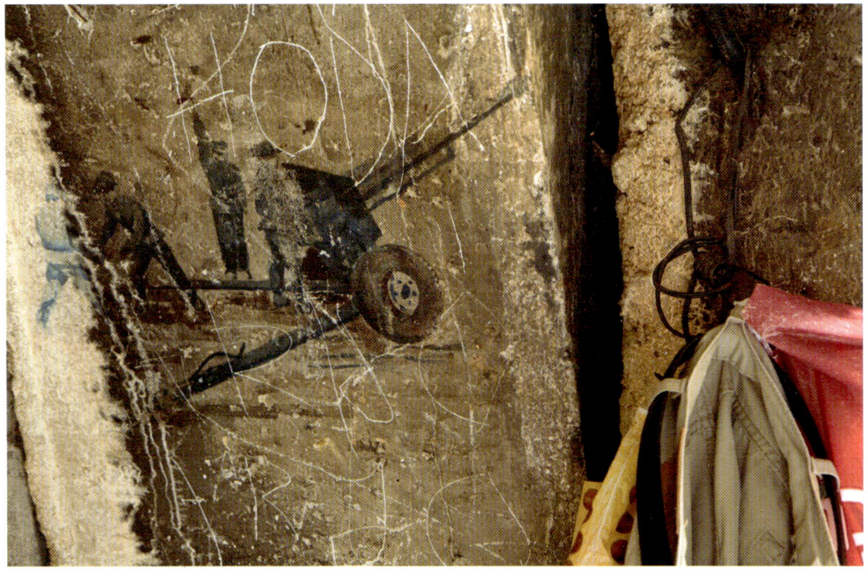

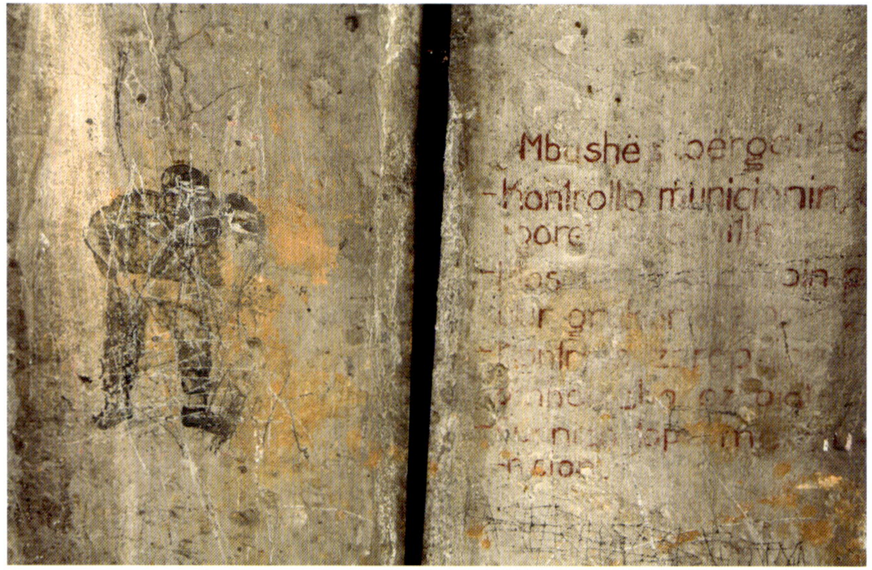

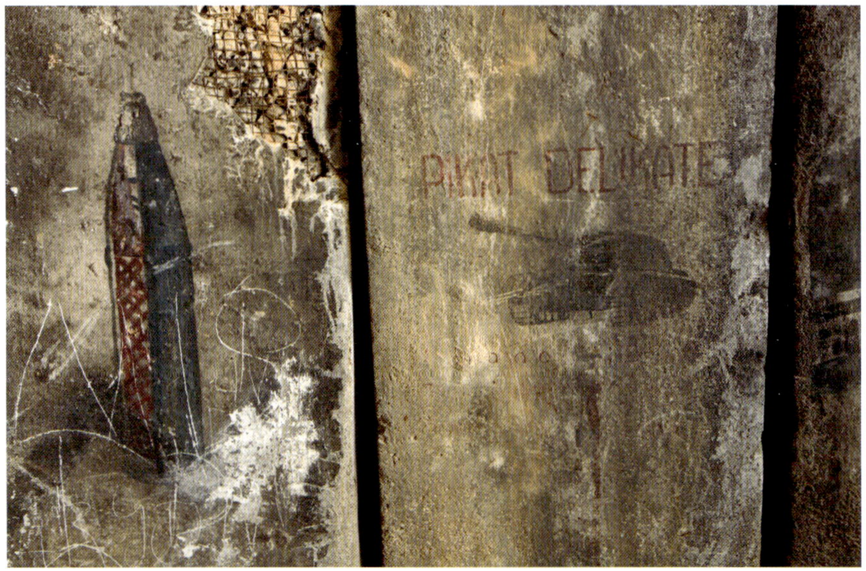
PIKAT DELIKATE

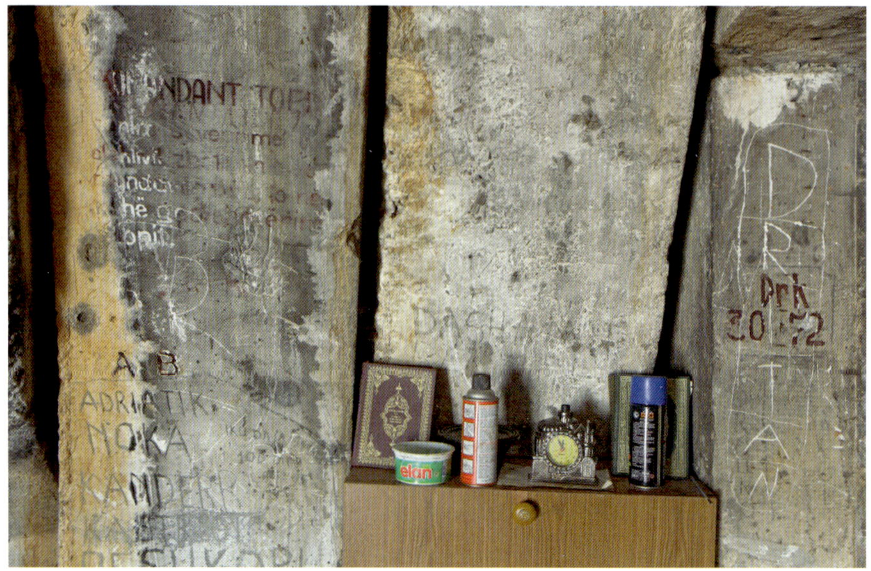
A B
ADRIATIK

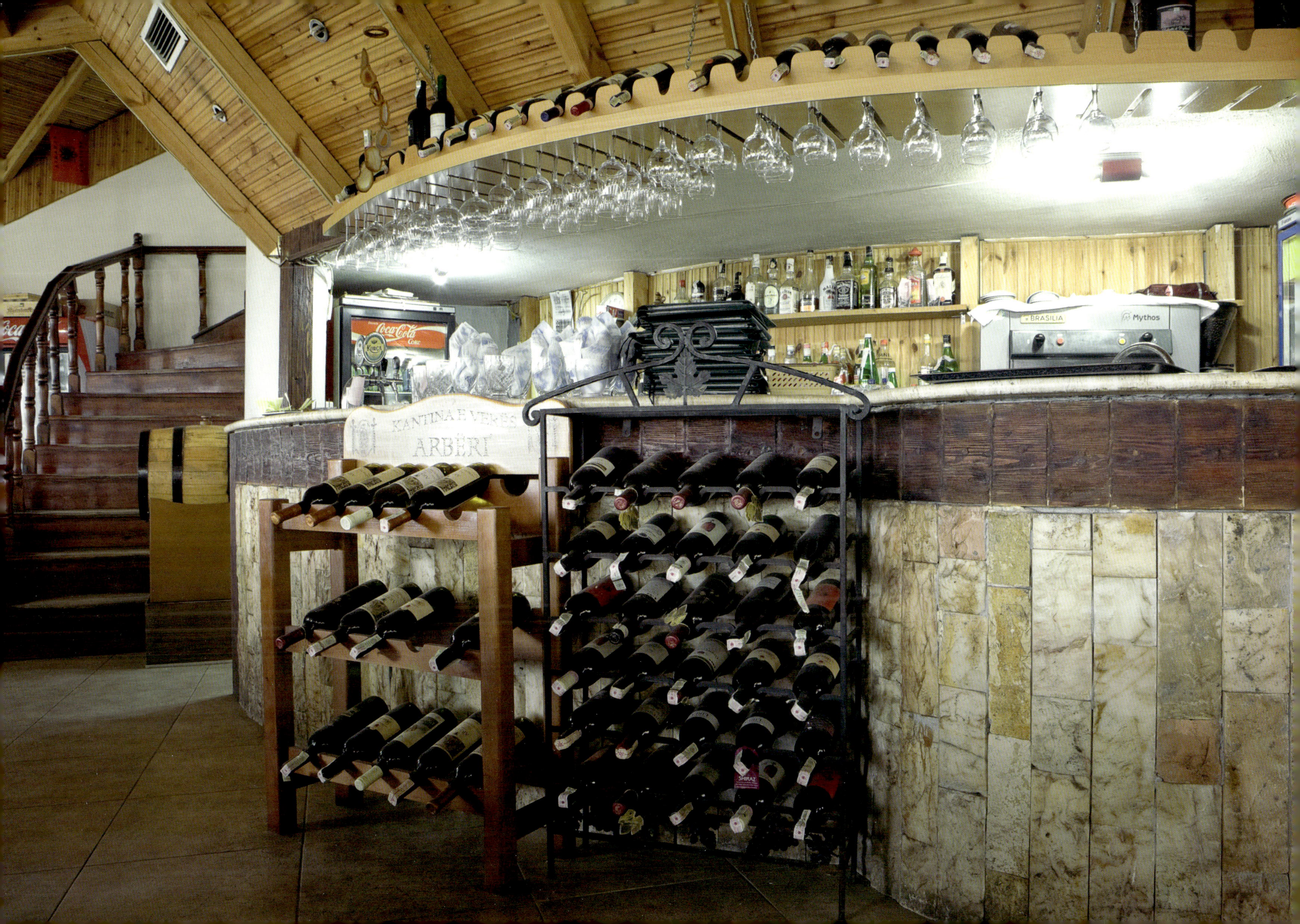
ARBËRI
Coca-Cola
BRASILIA
Mythos

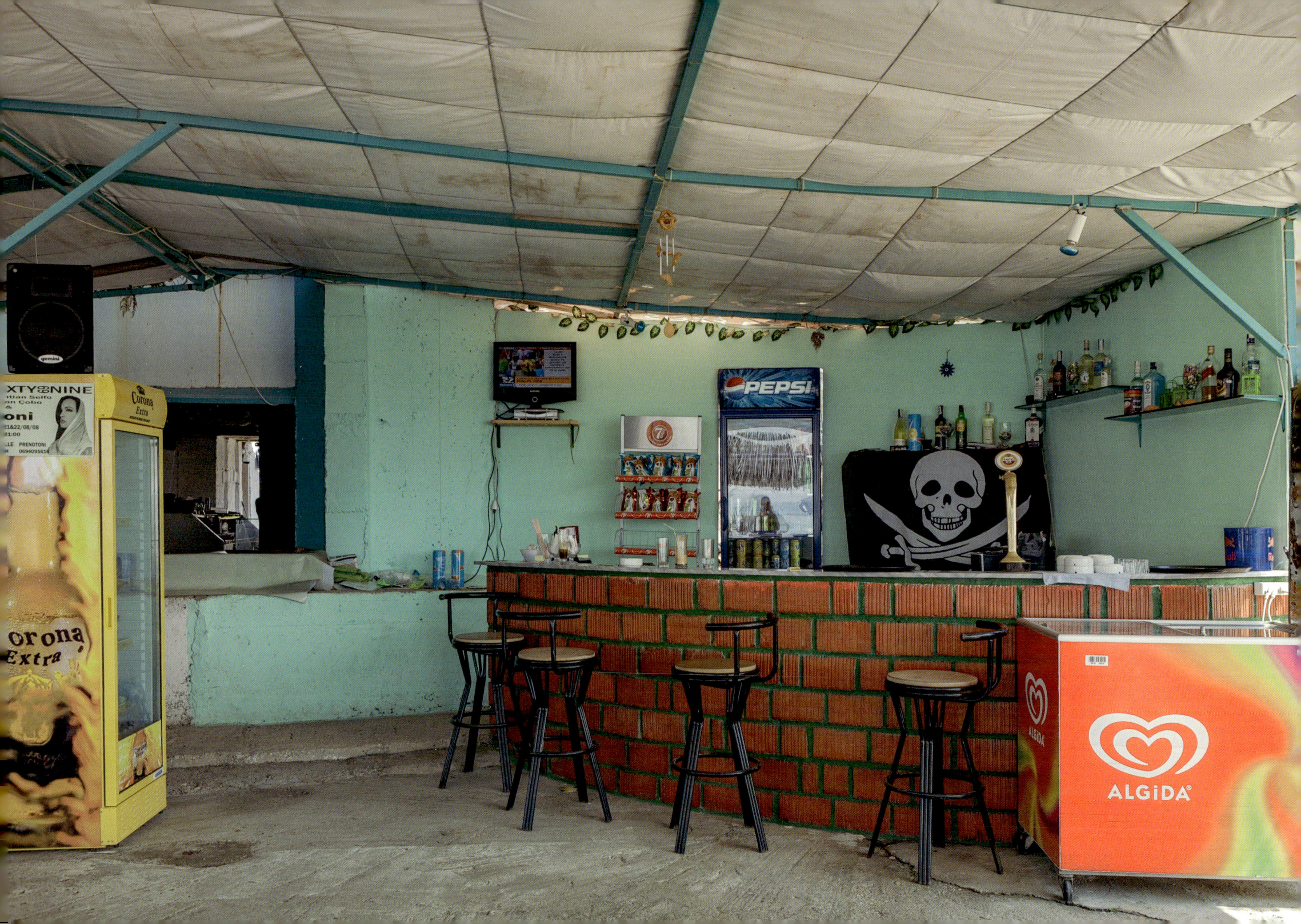
Corona
Extra
PEPSI
Corona
Extra
ALGIDA
ALGIDA

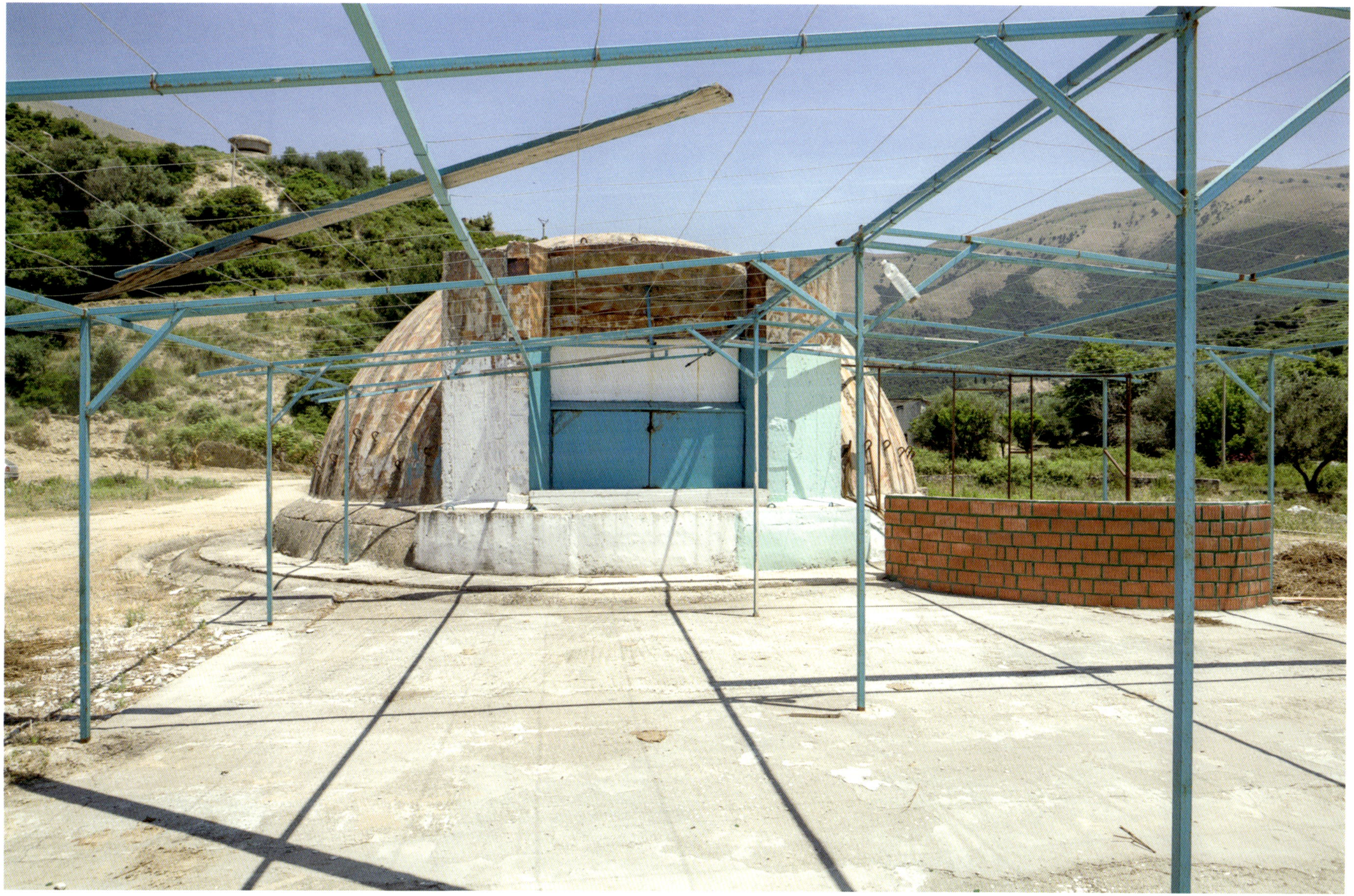

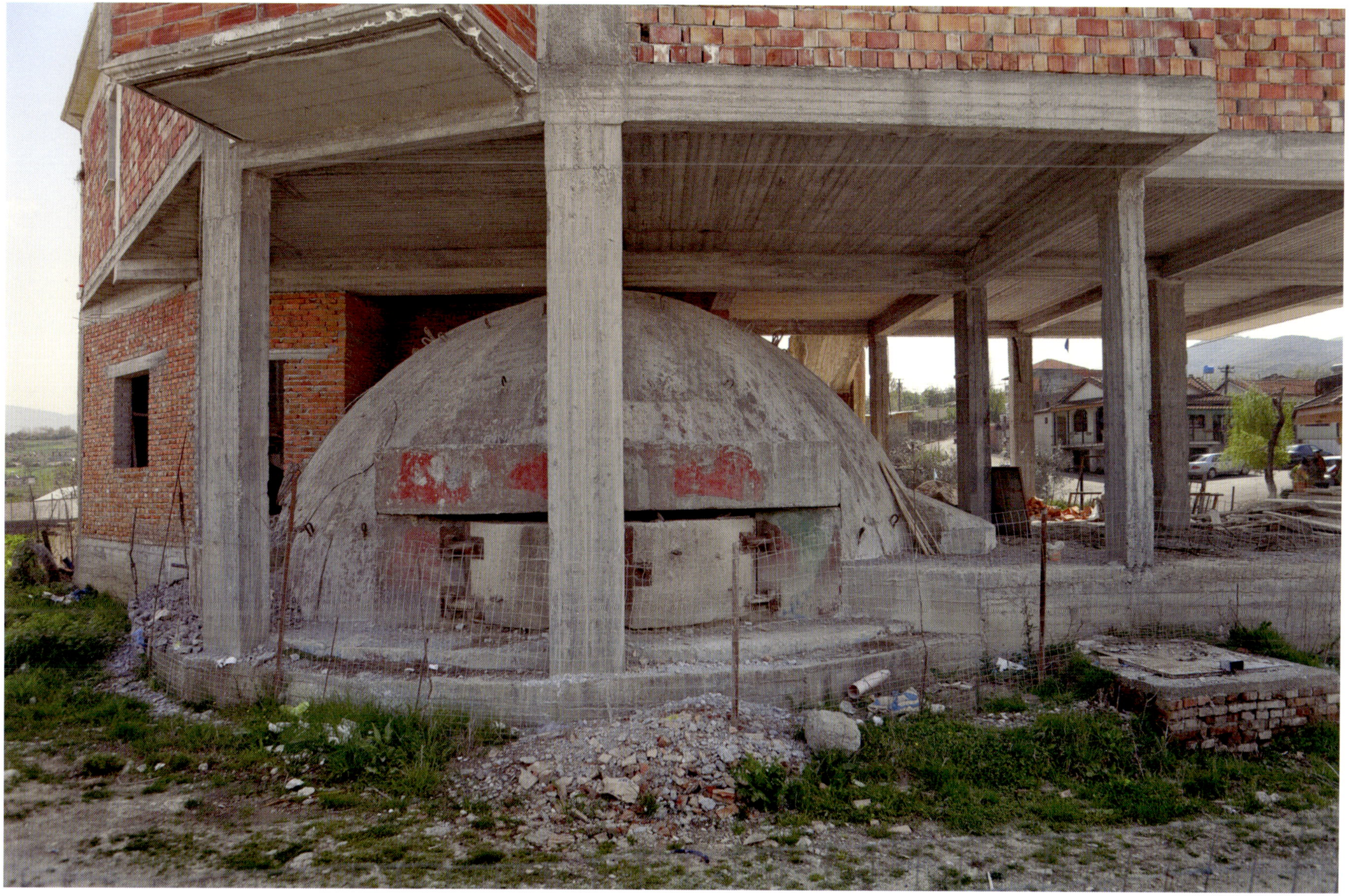

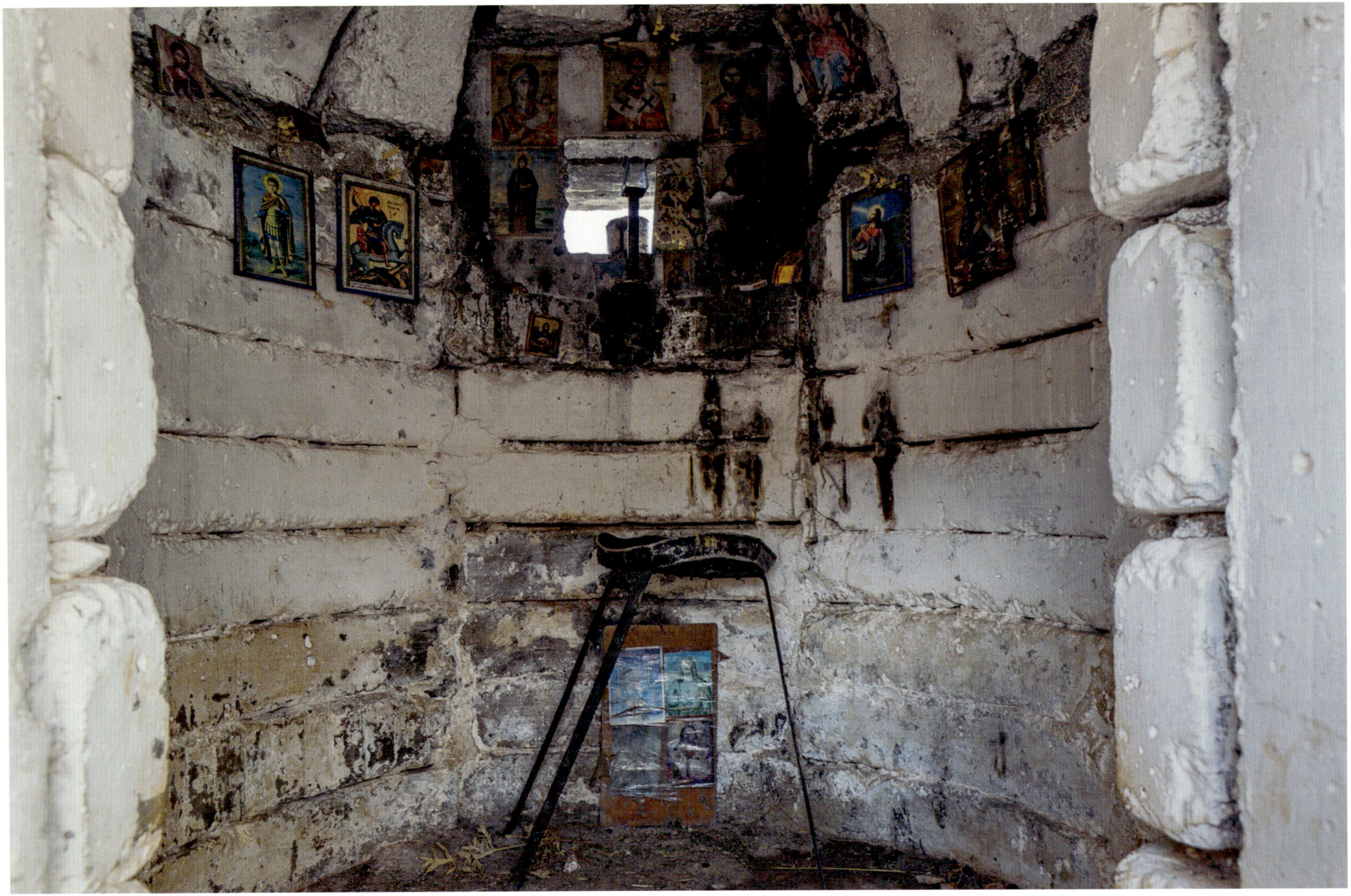

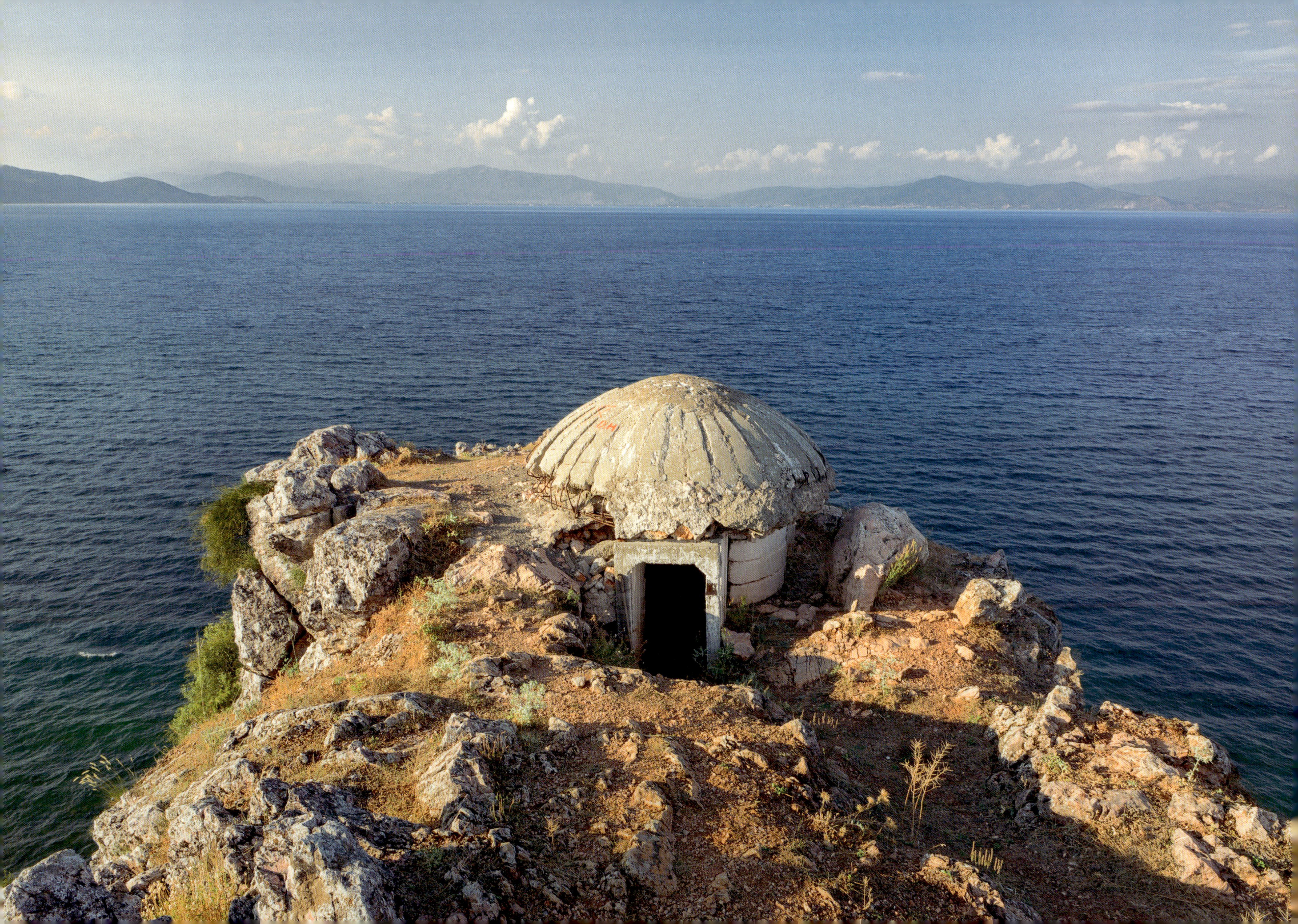

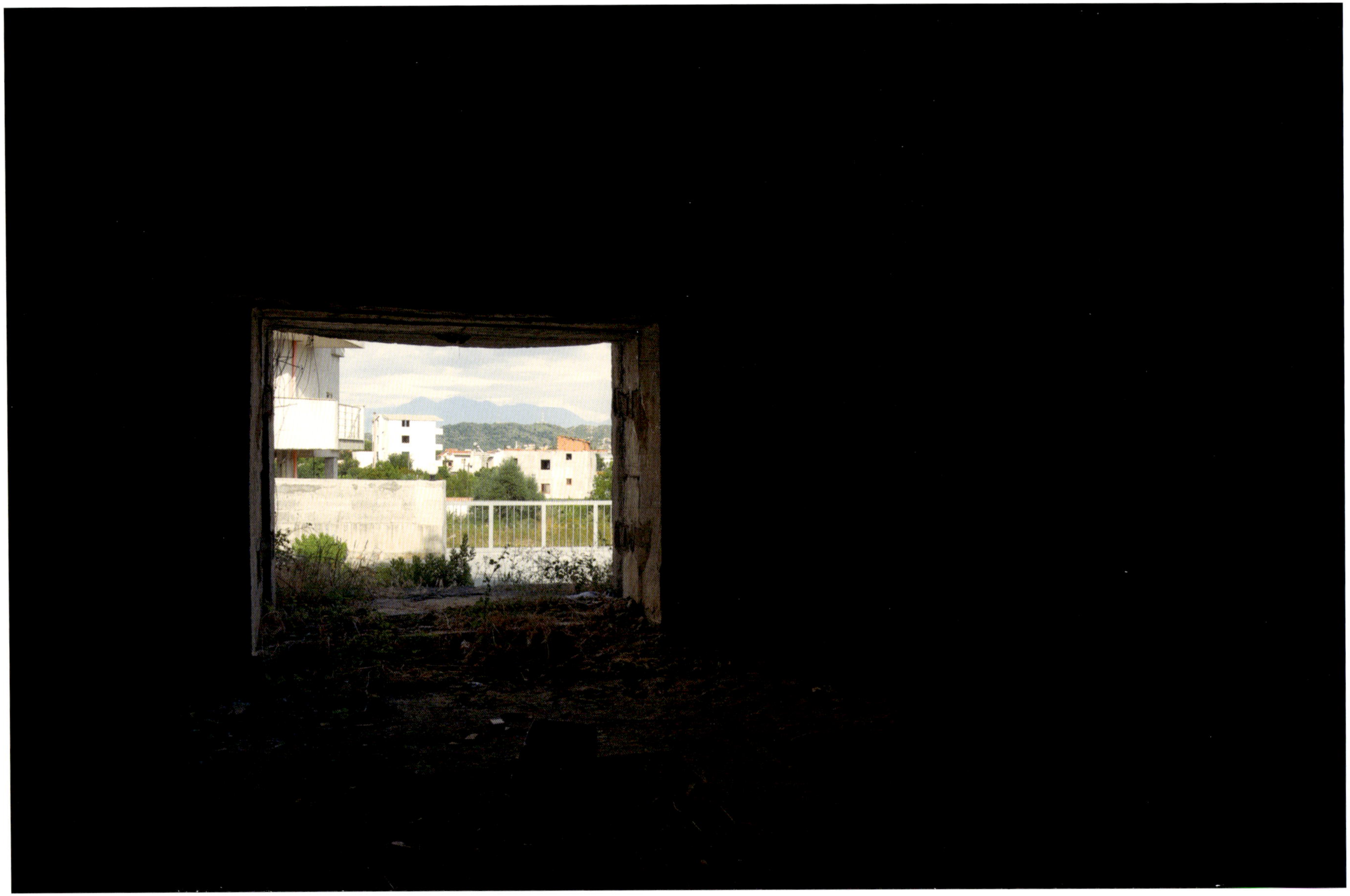

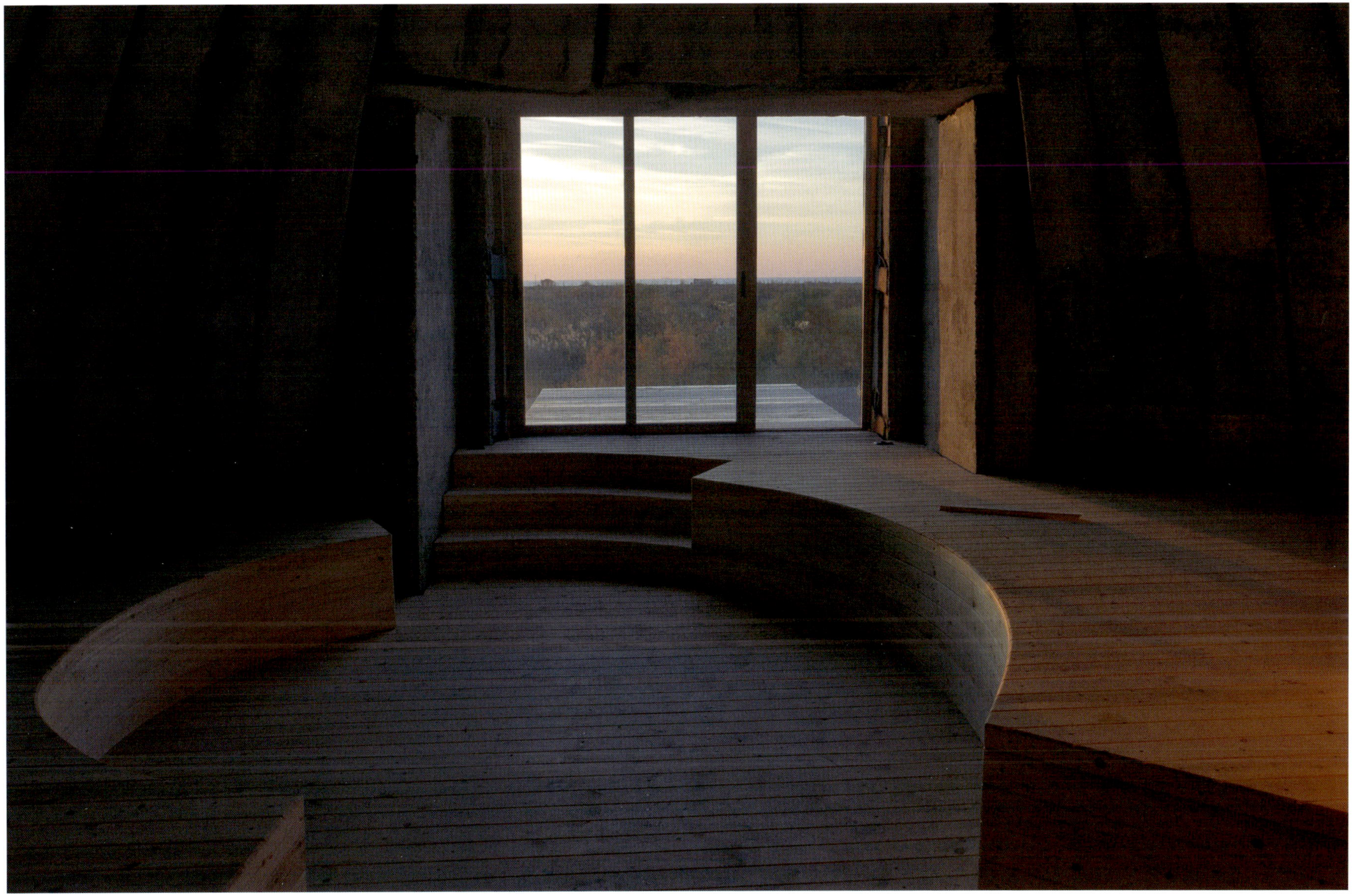

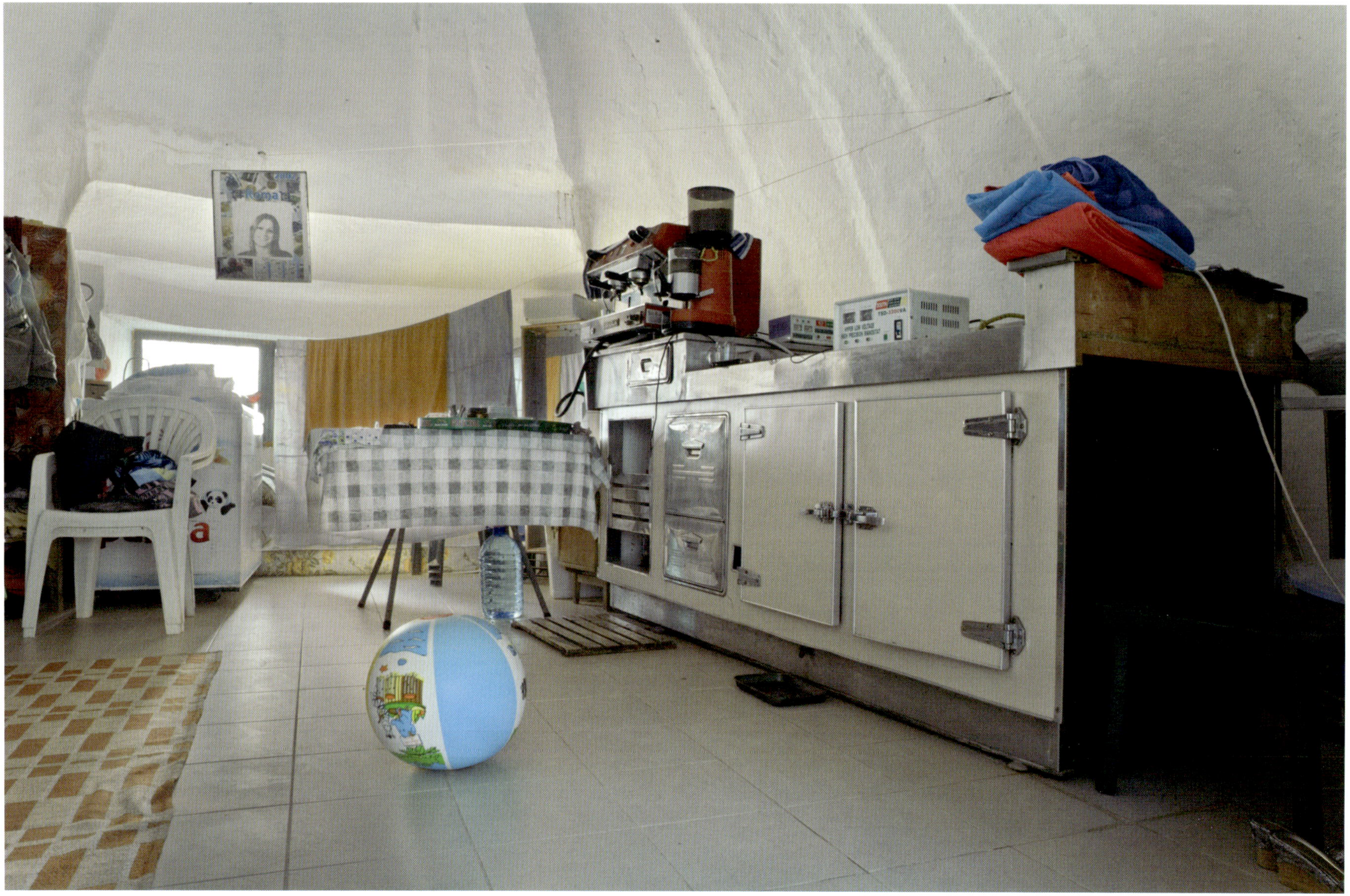

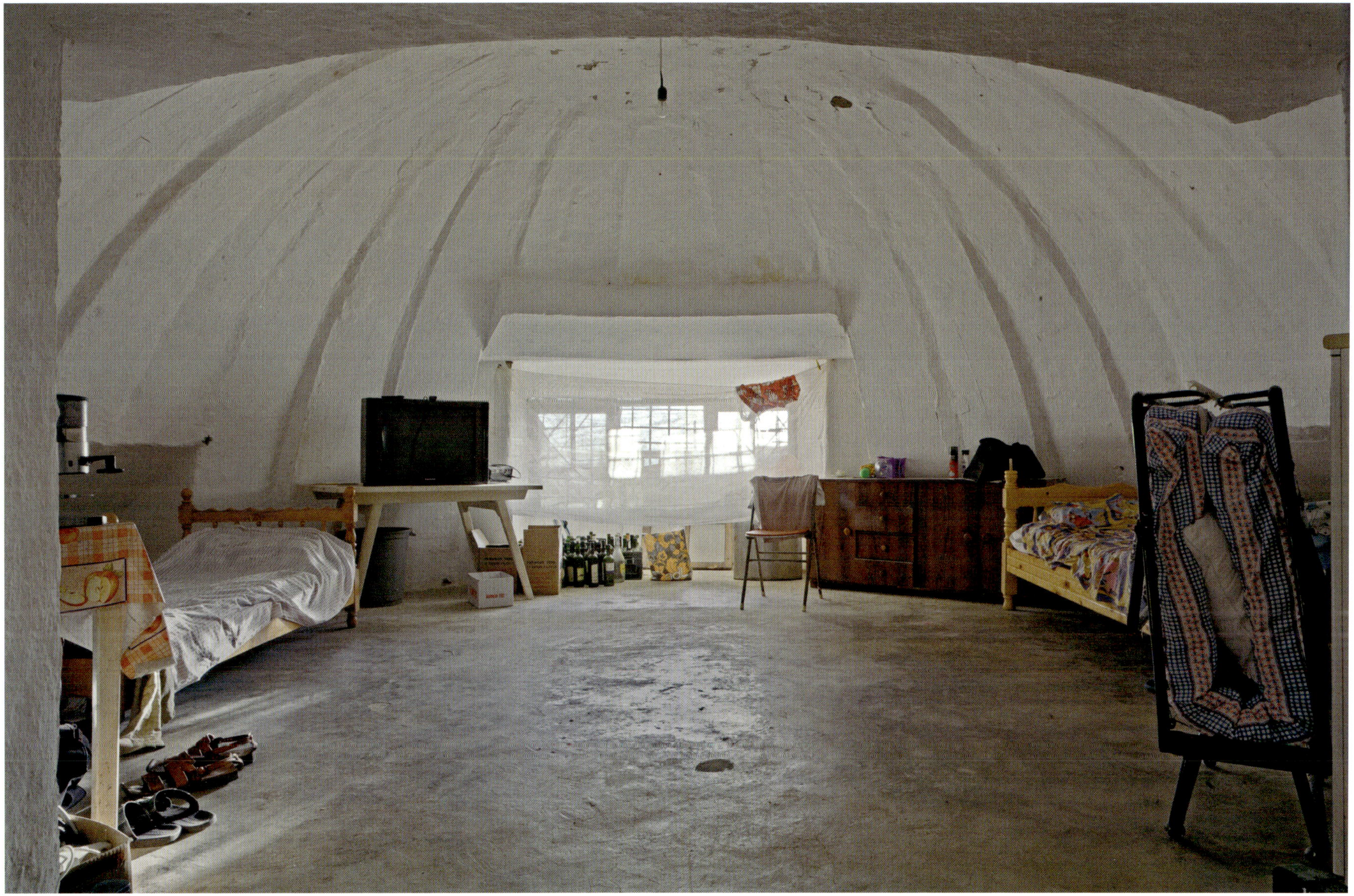

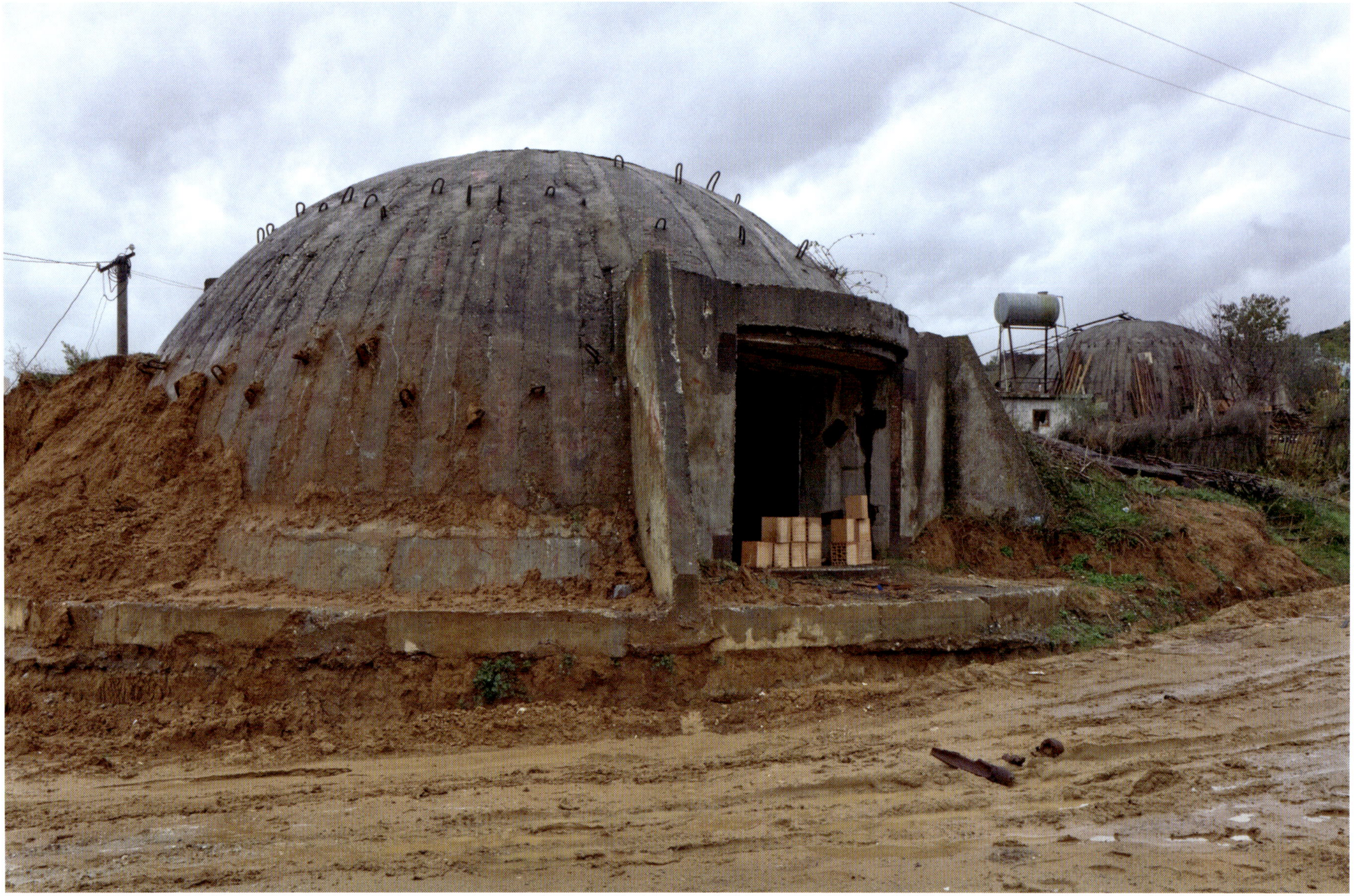

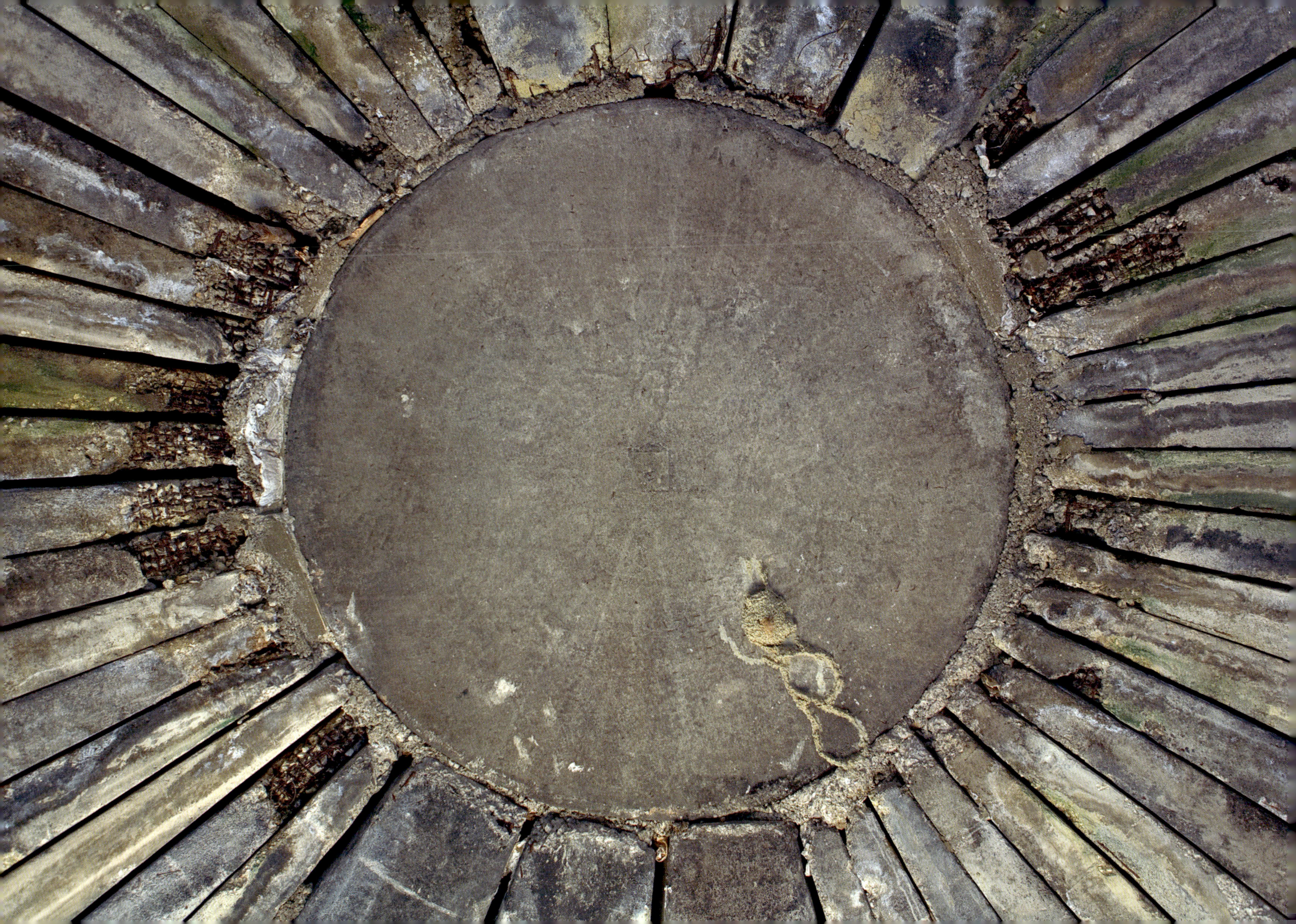

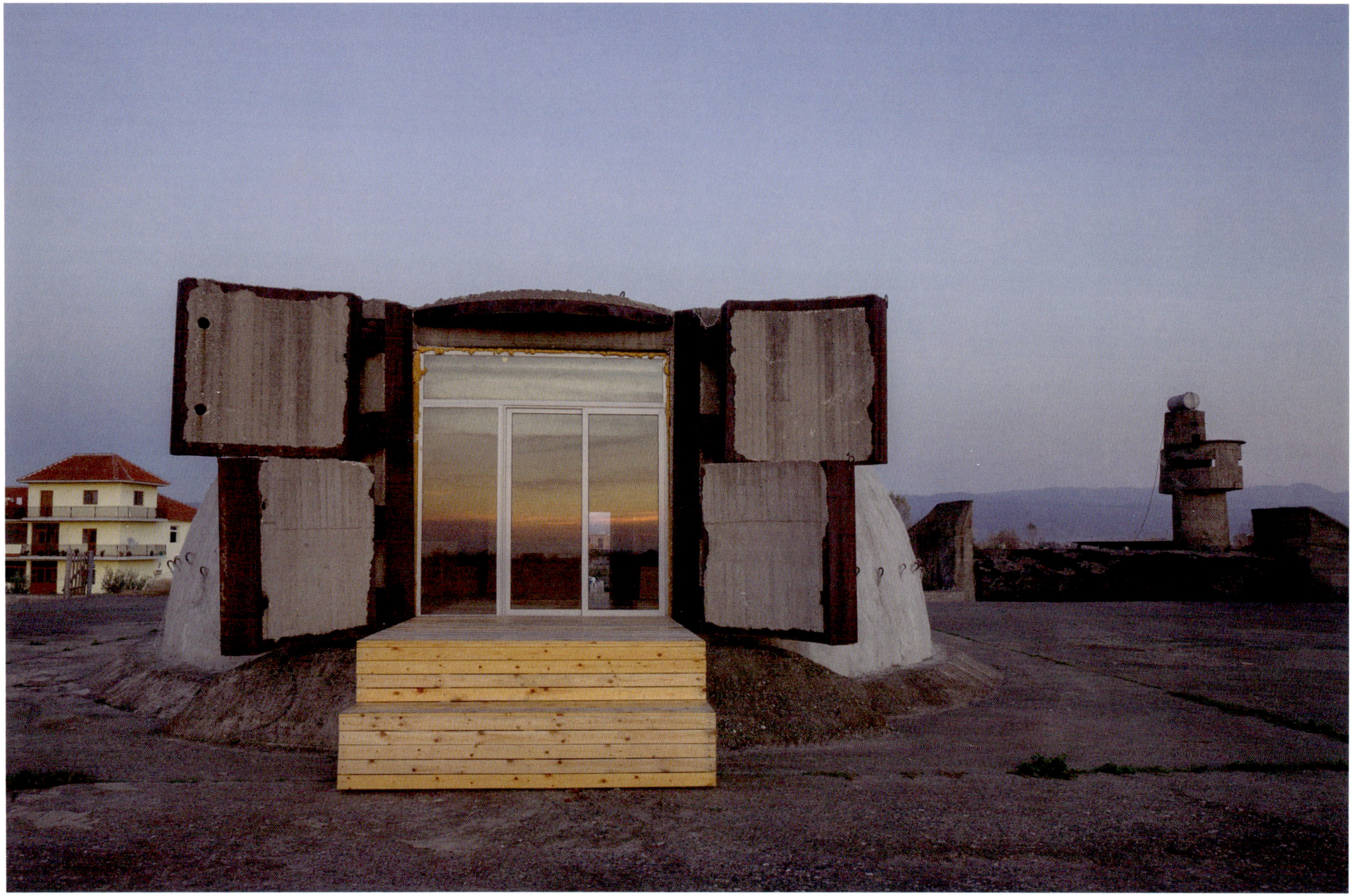

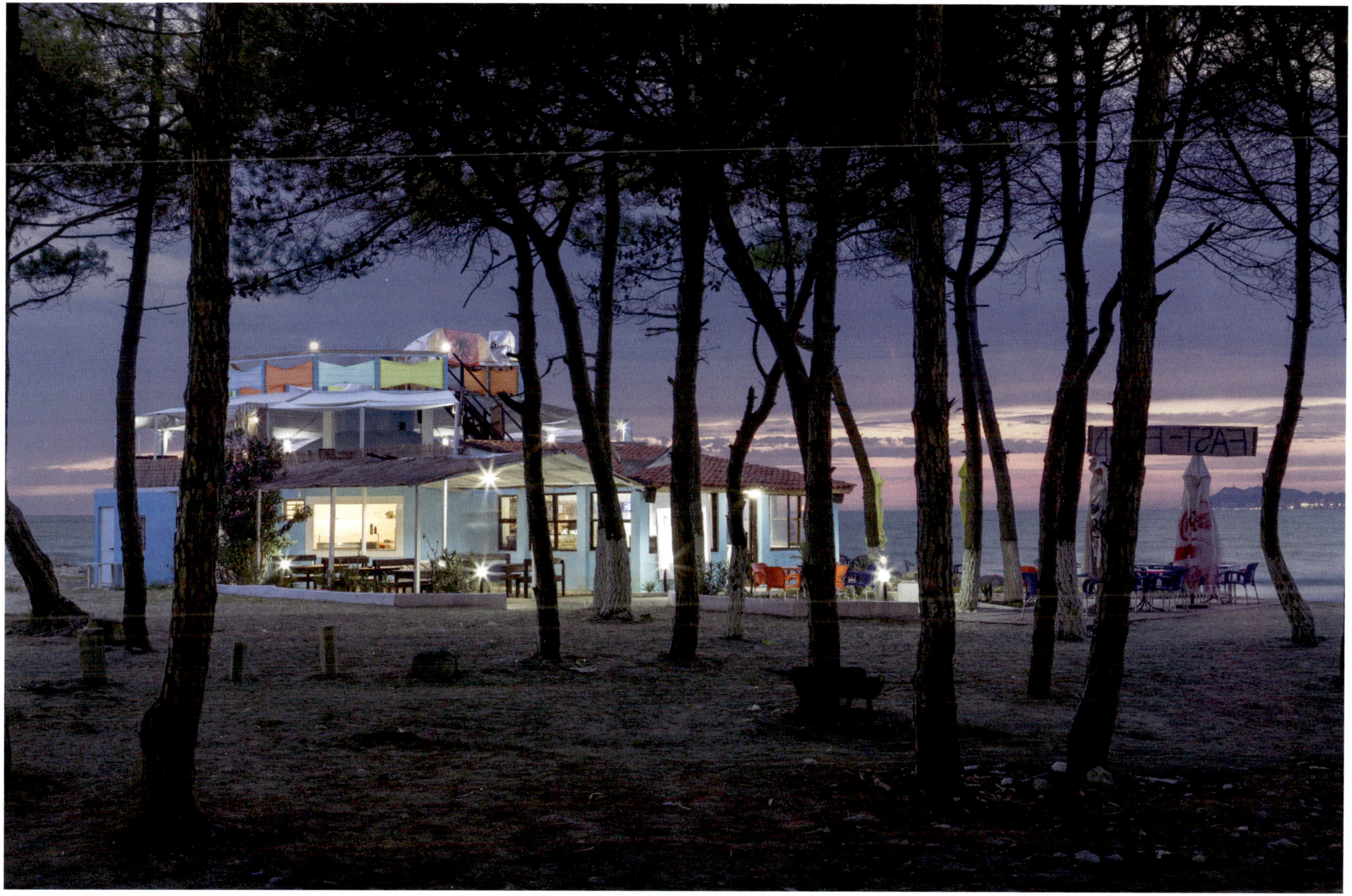

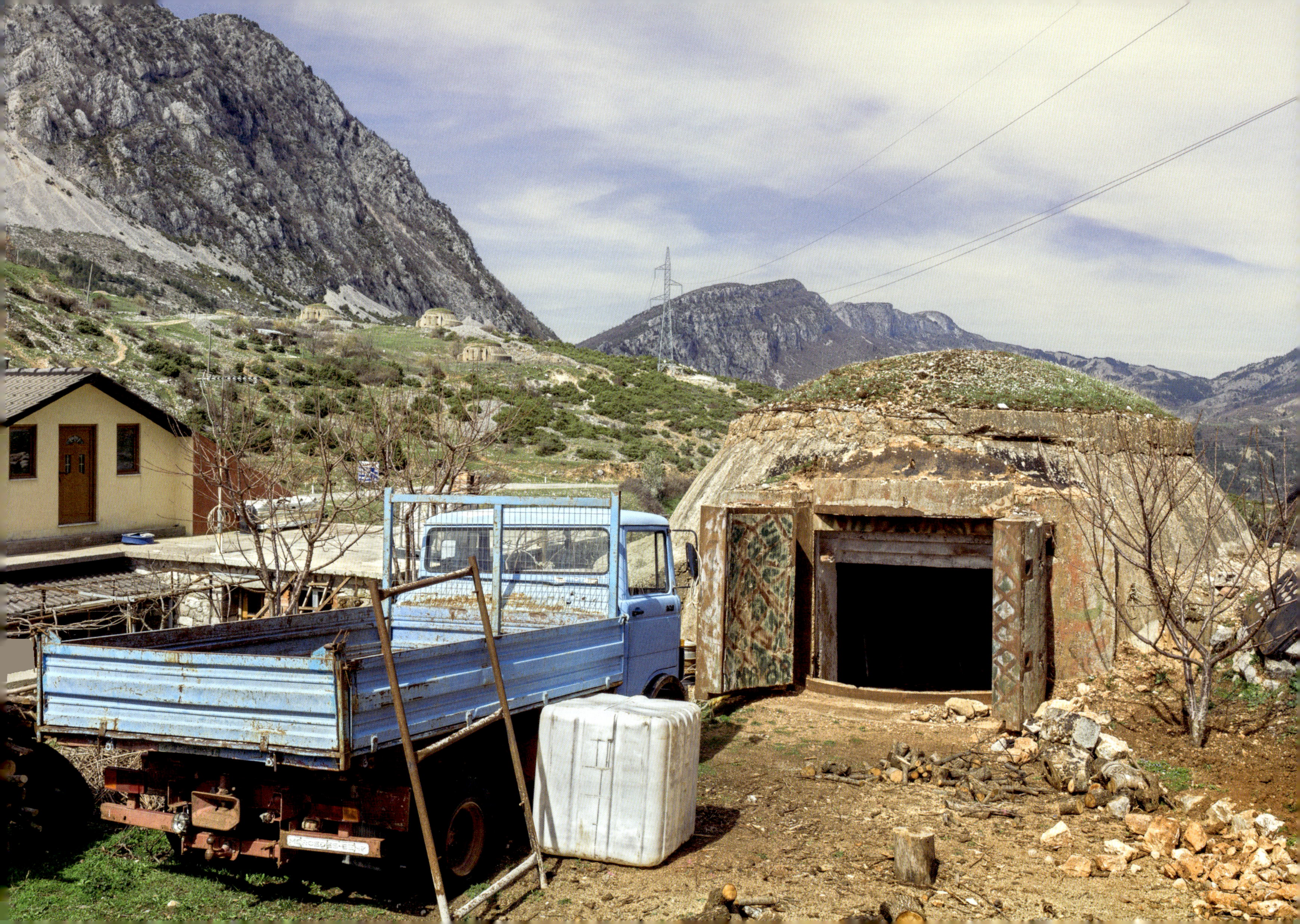

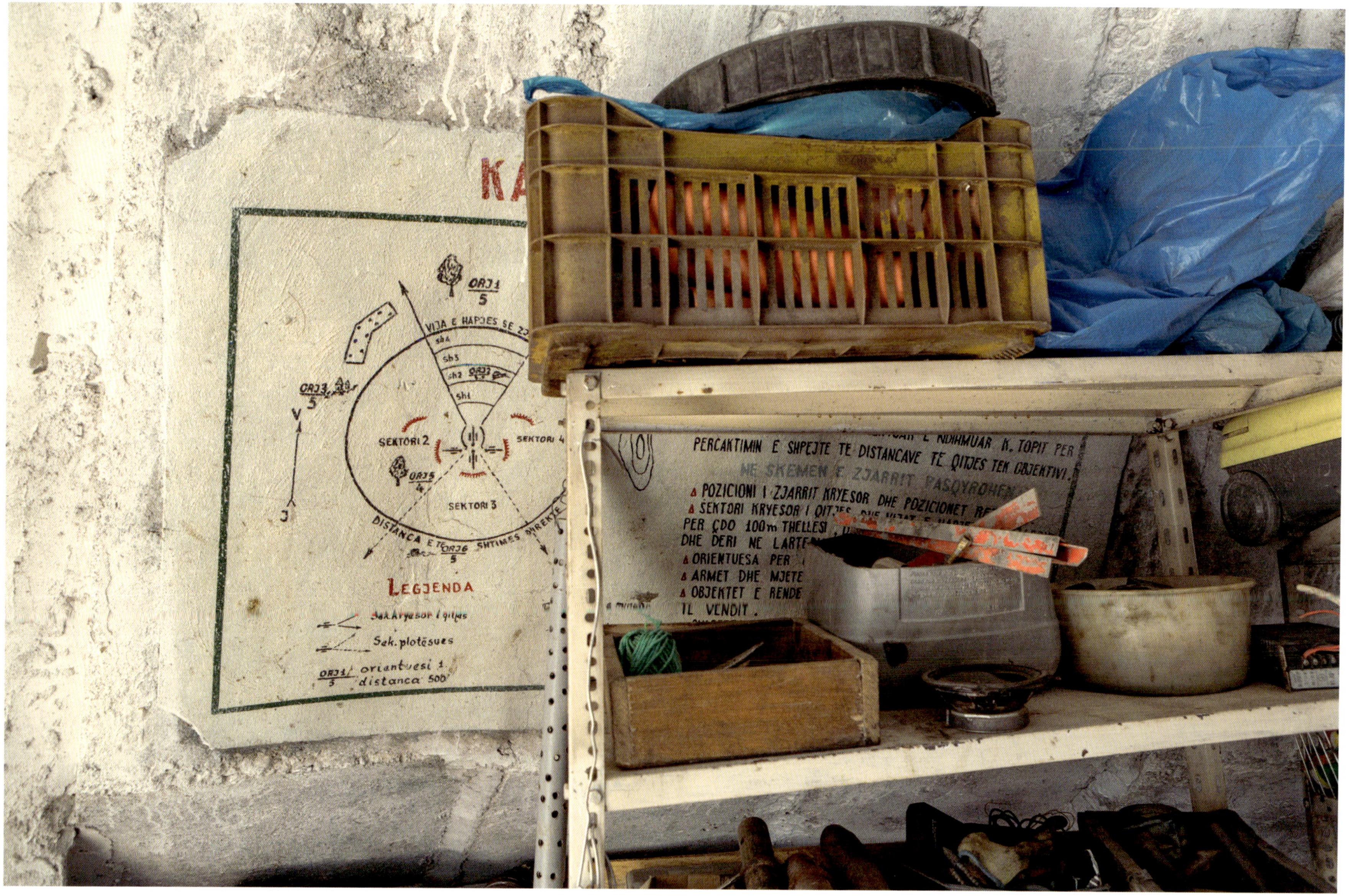
ORJ 1
5
VIJA E HAPJES SE ZJ
sh4
sh3
sh2
sh1
ORJ 3
5
V
J
SEKTORI 2
SEKTORI 4
ORJ 5
4
SEKTORI 3
DISTANCA E TE SHTIMES DIREKTE
ORJ 6
5
LEGJENDA
Sek. plotësues
ORJ 1/5 orientuesi 1.
distanca 500
PERCAKTIMIN E SHPEJTE TE DISTANCAVE TE QITJES TEK OBJEKTIVI.
NE SKEMEN E ZJARRIT PASQYROHEN
POZICIONI I ZJARRIT KRYESOR DHE POZICIONET
SEKTORI KRYESOR I QITJES
PER ÇDO 100m THELLESI
DHE DERI NE
ORIENTUESA PER
ARMET DHE MJETE
OBJEKTET E RENDE
TE VENDIT.

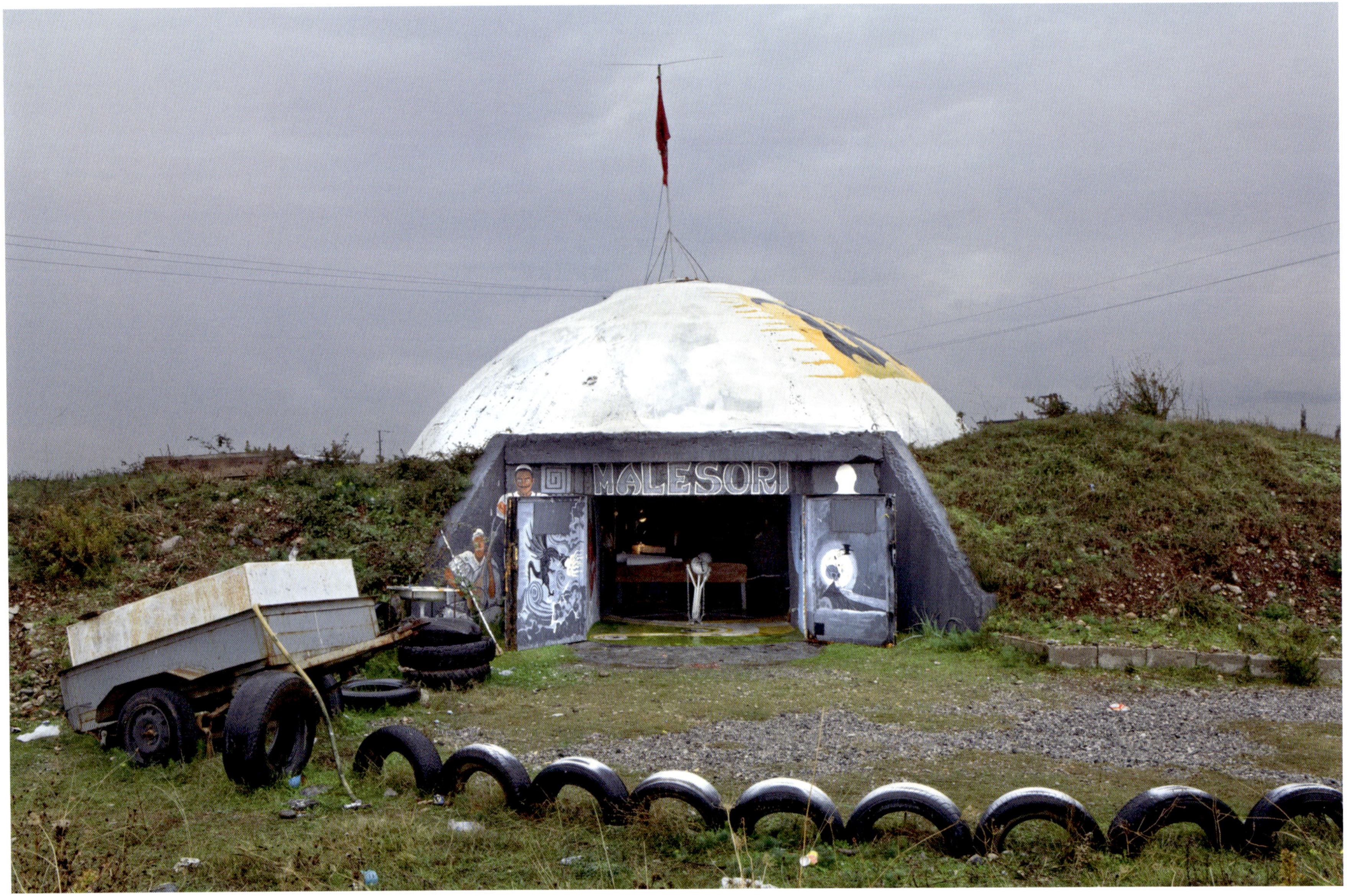
MALESORI

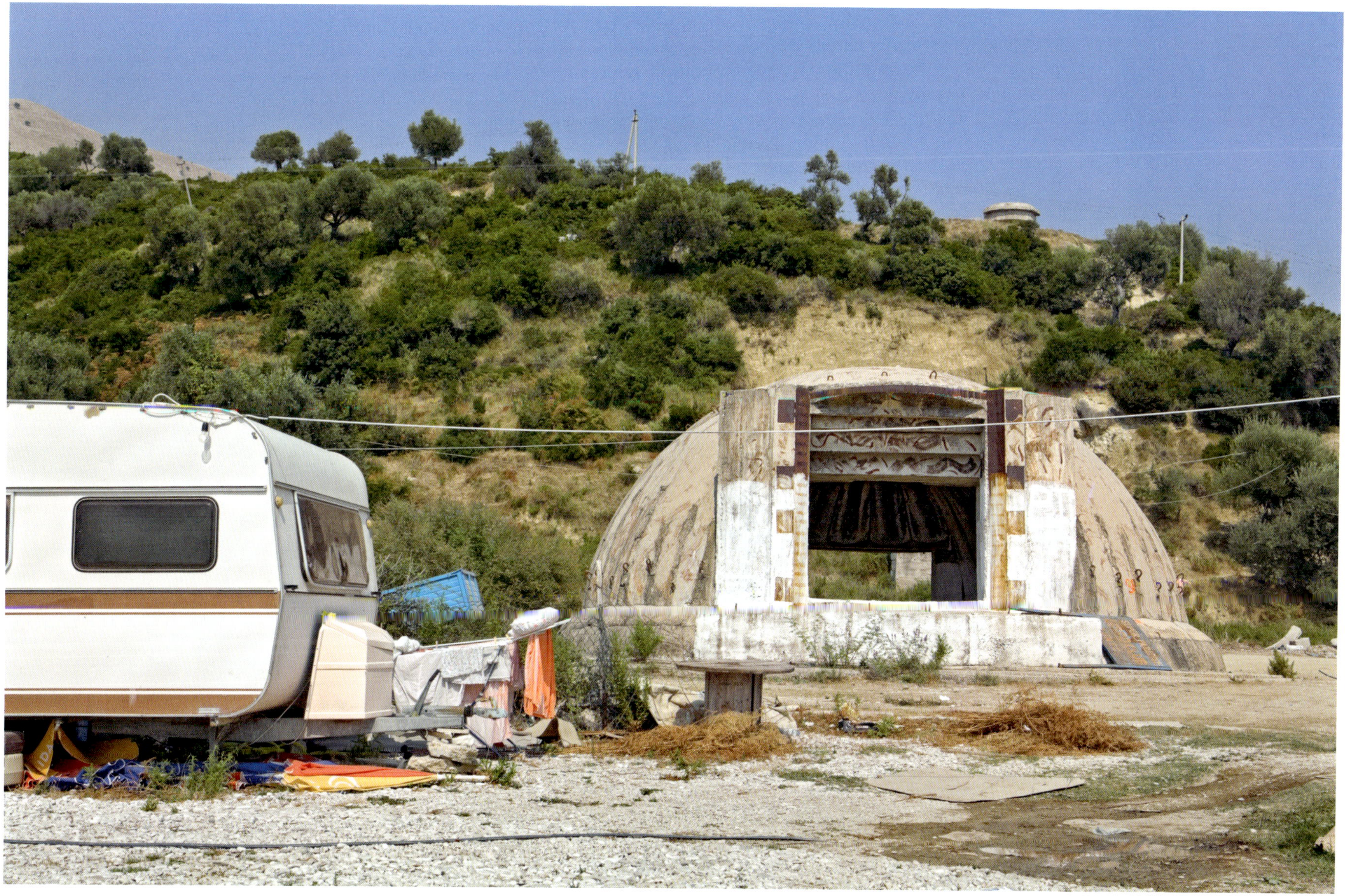

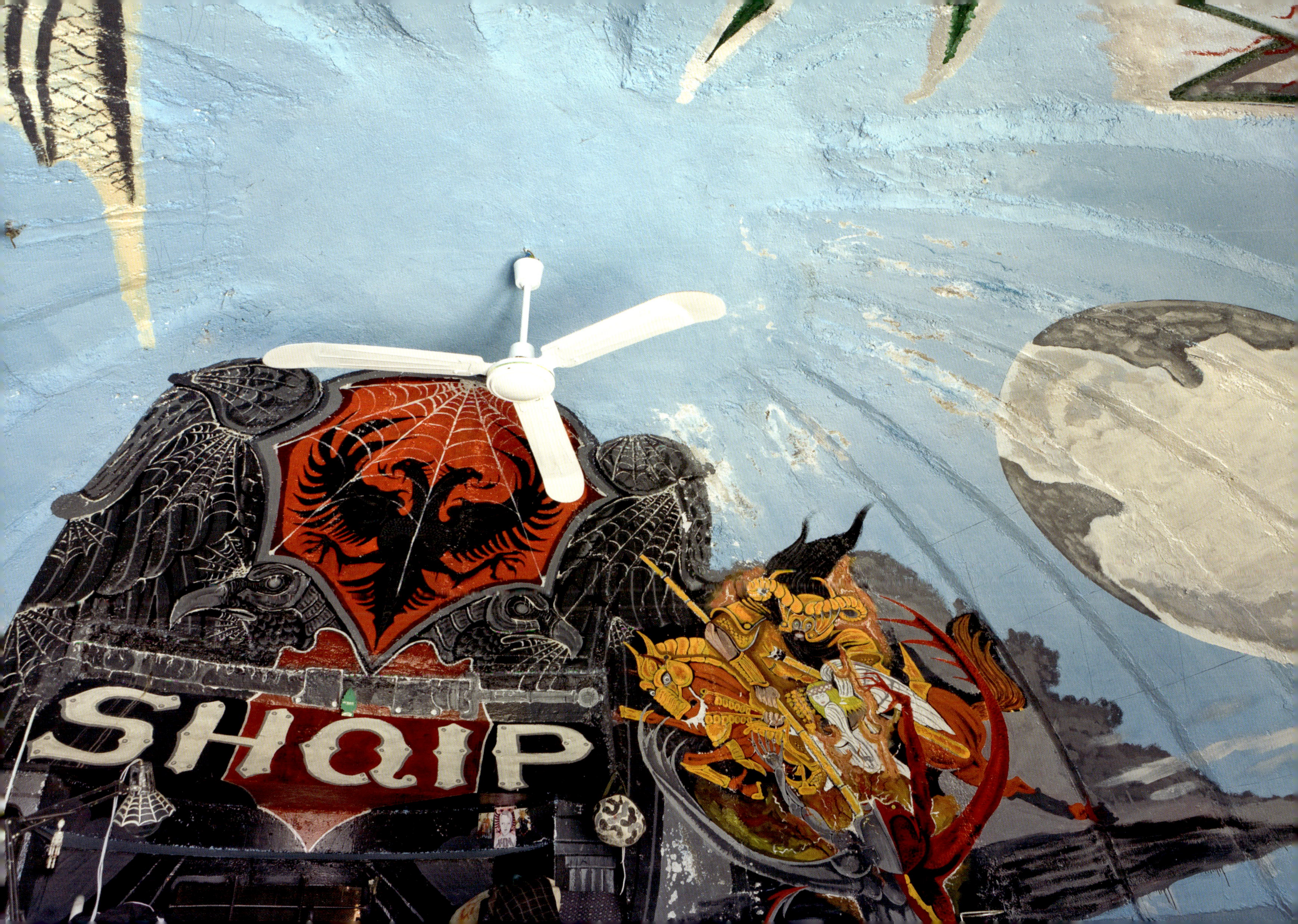
SHQIP

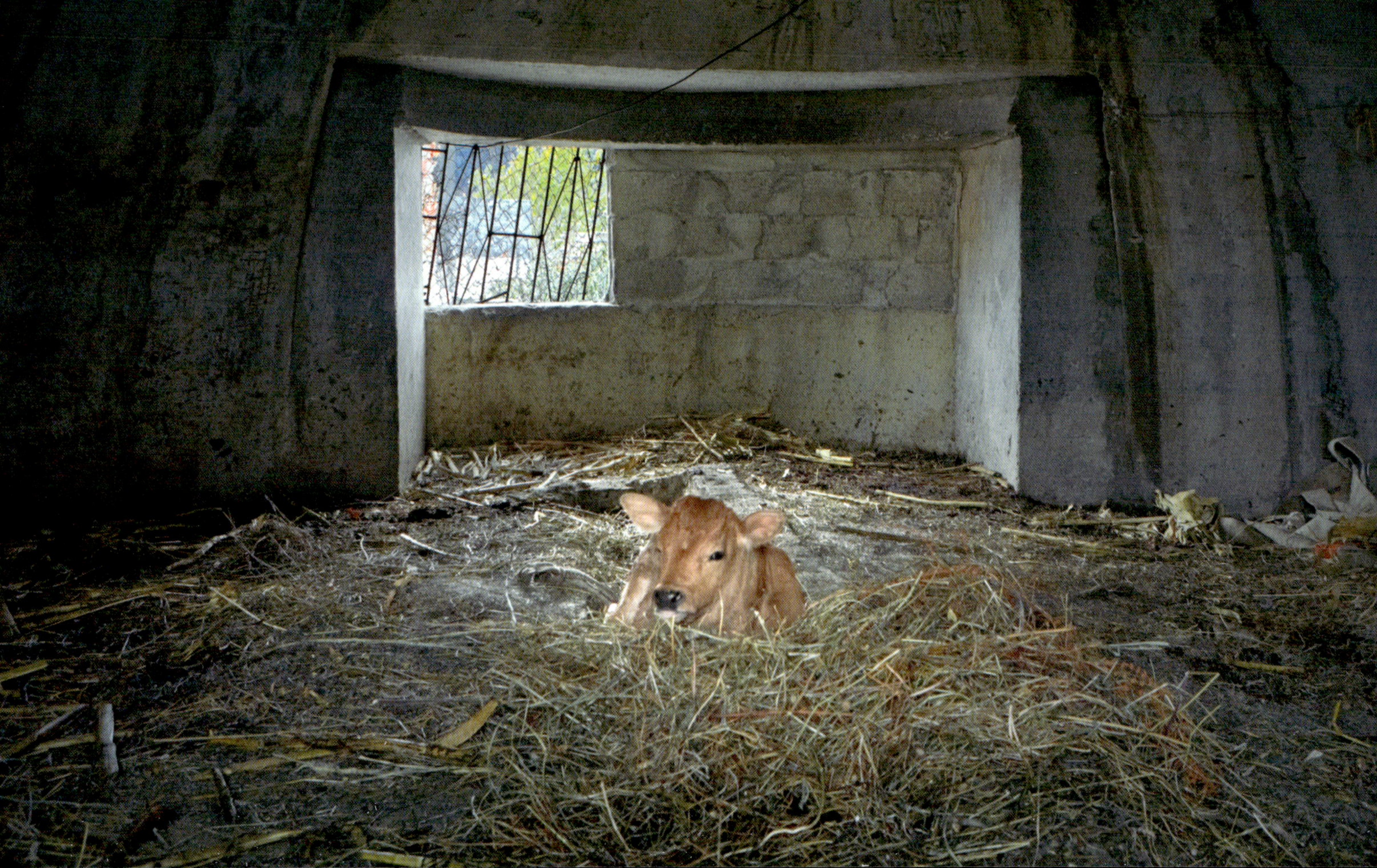

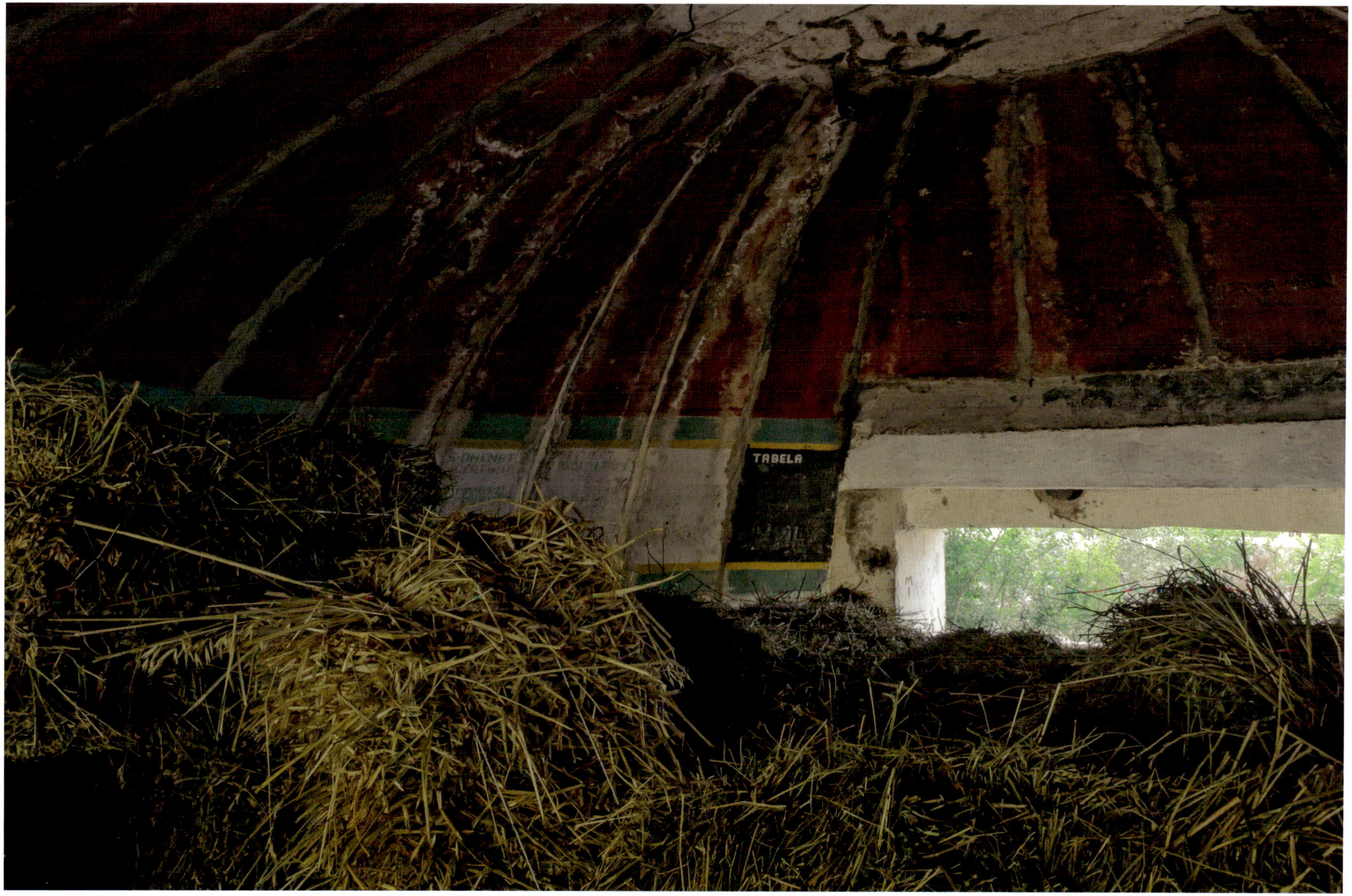
TABELA

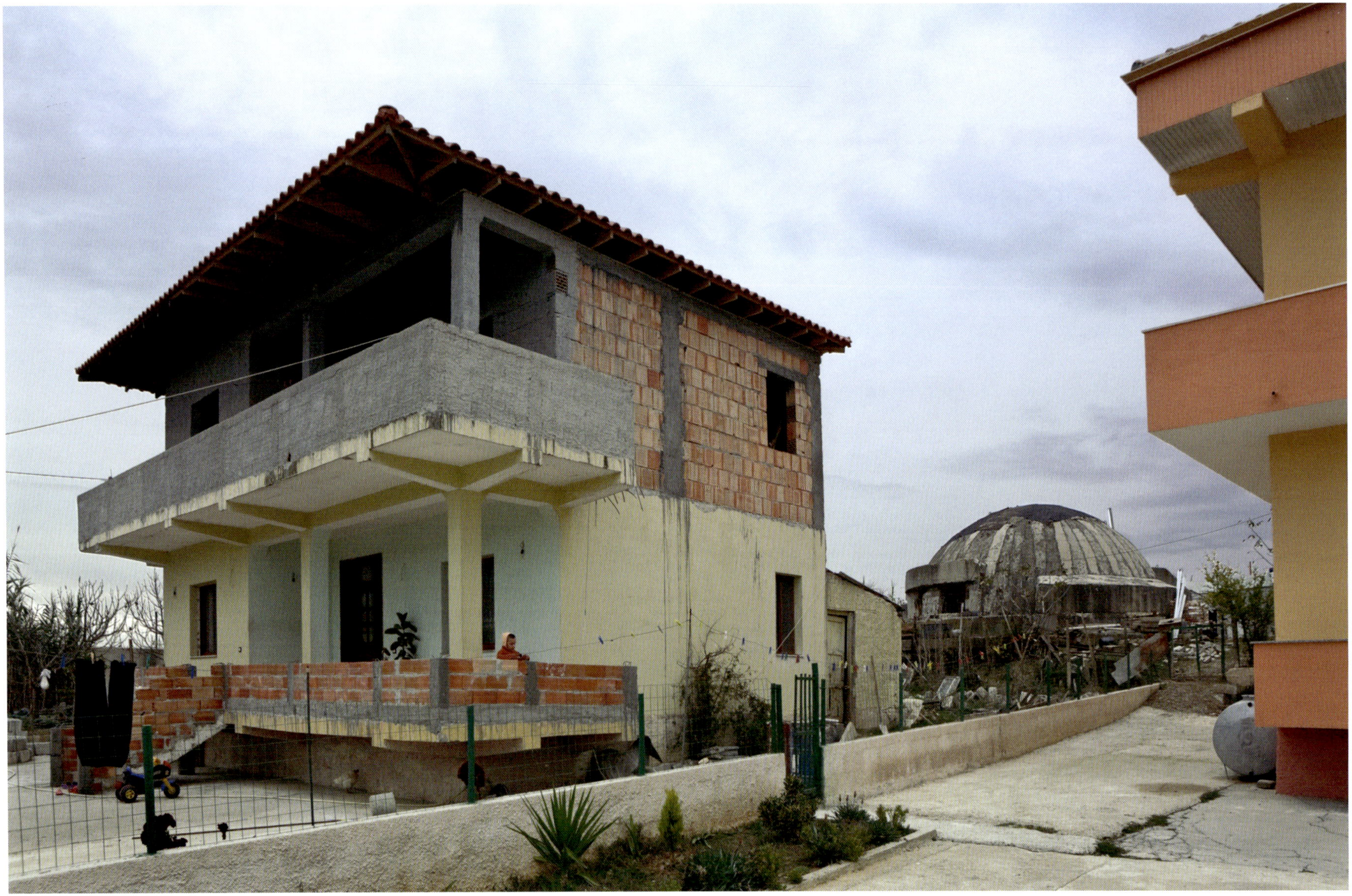

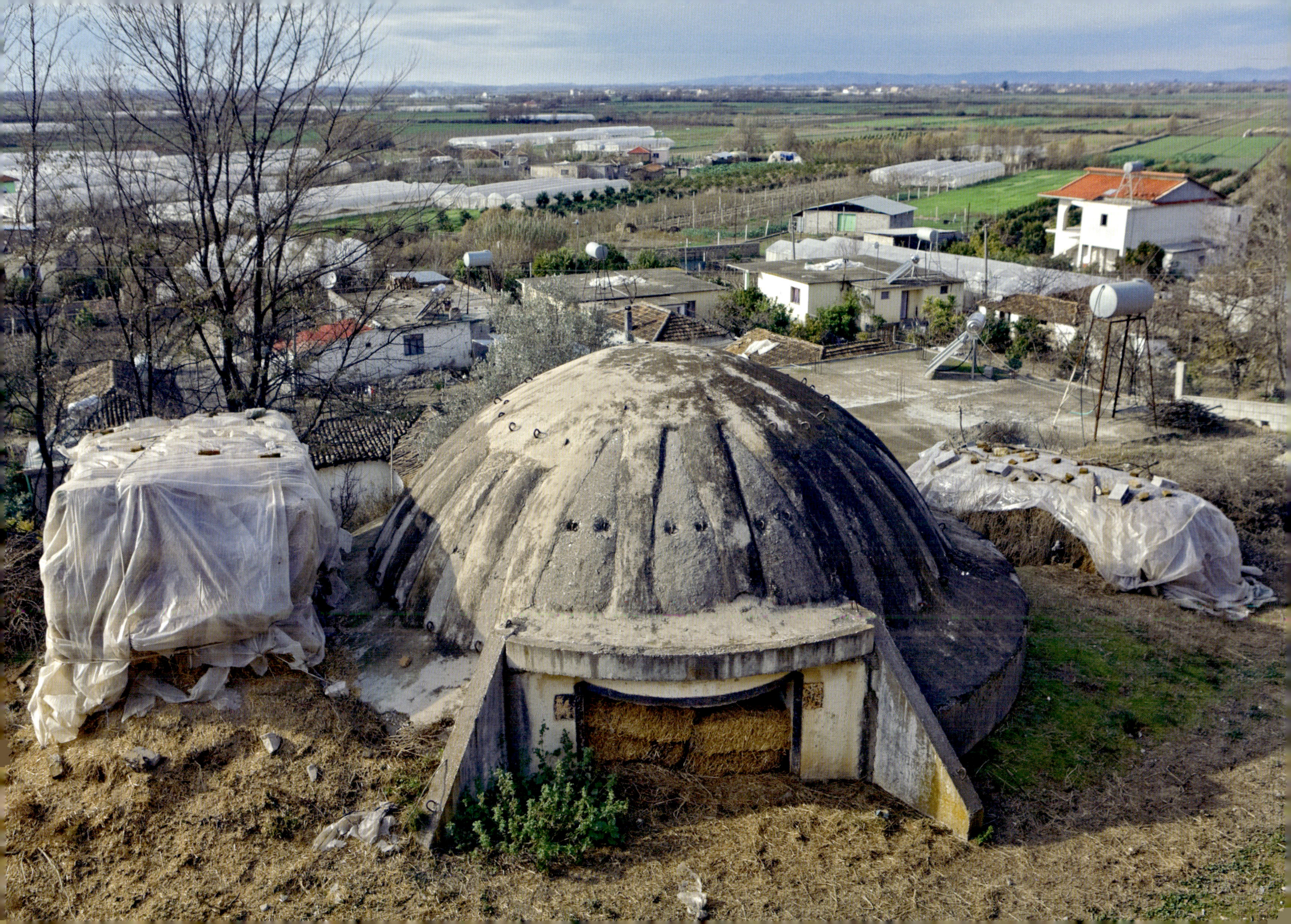

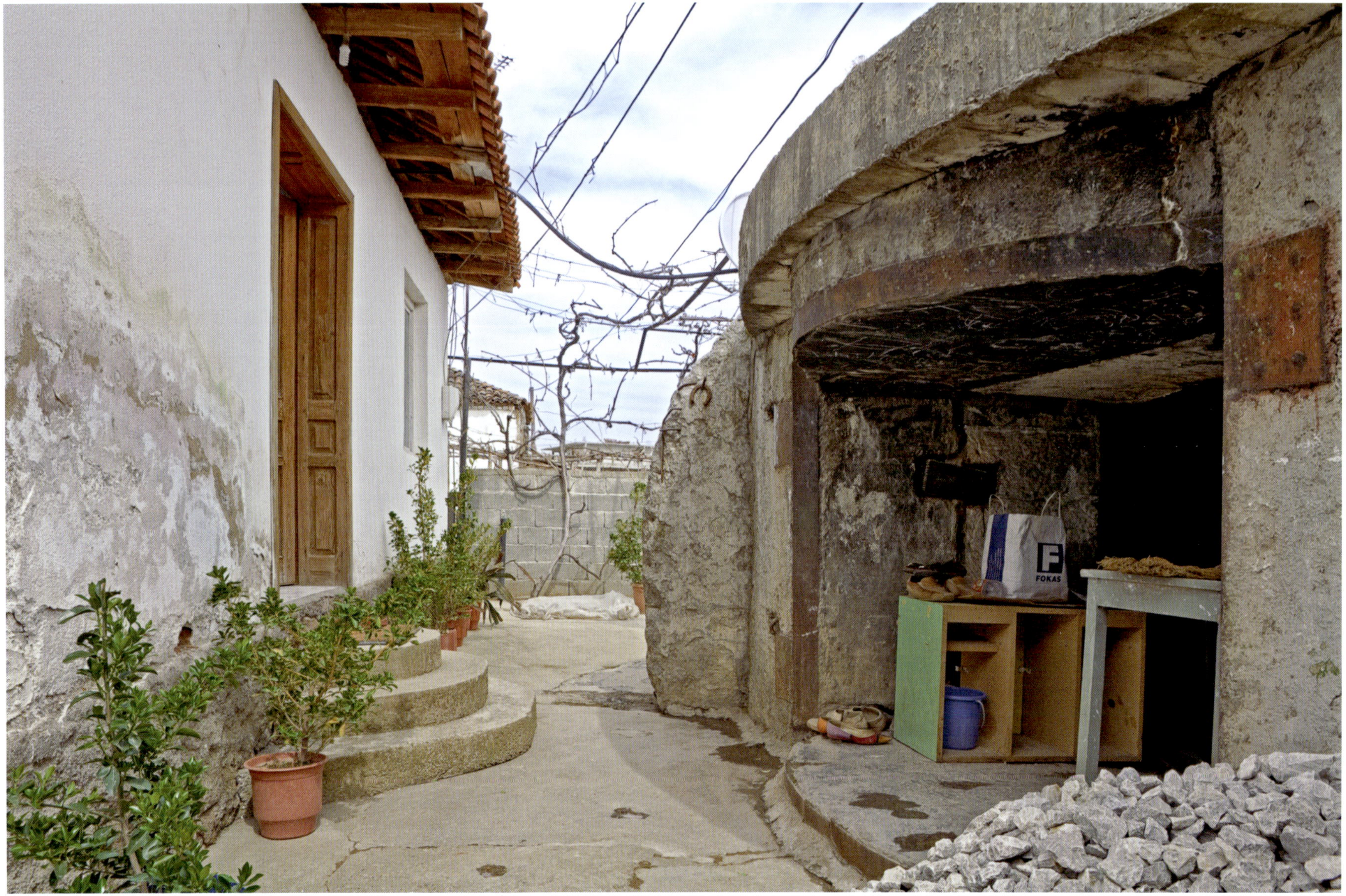
F
FOKAS

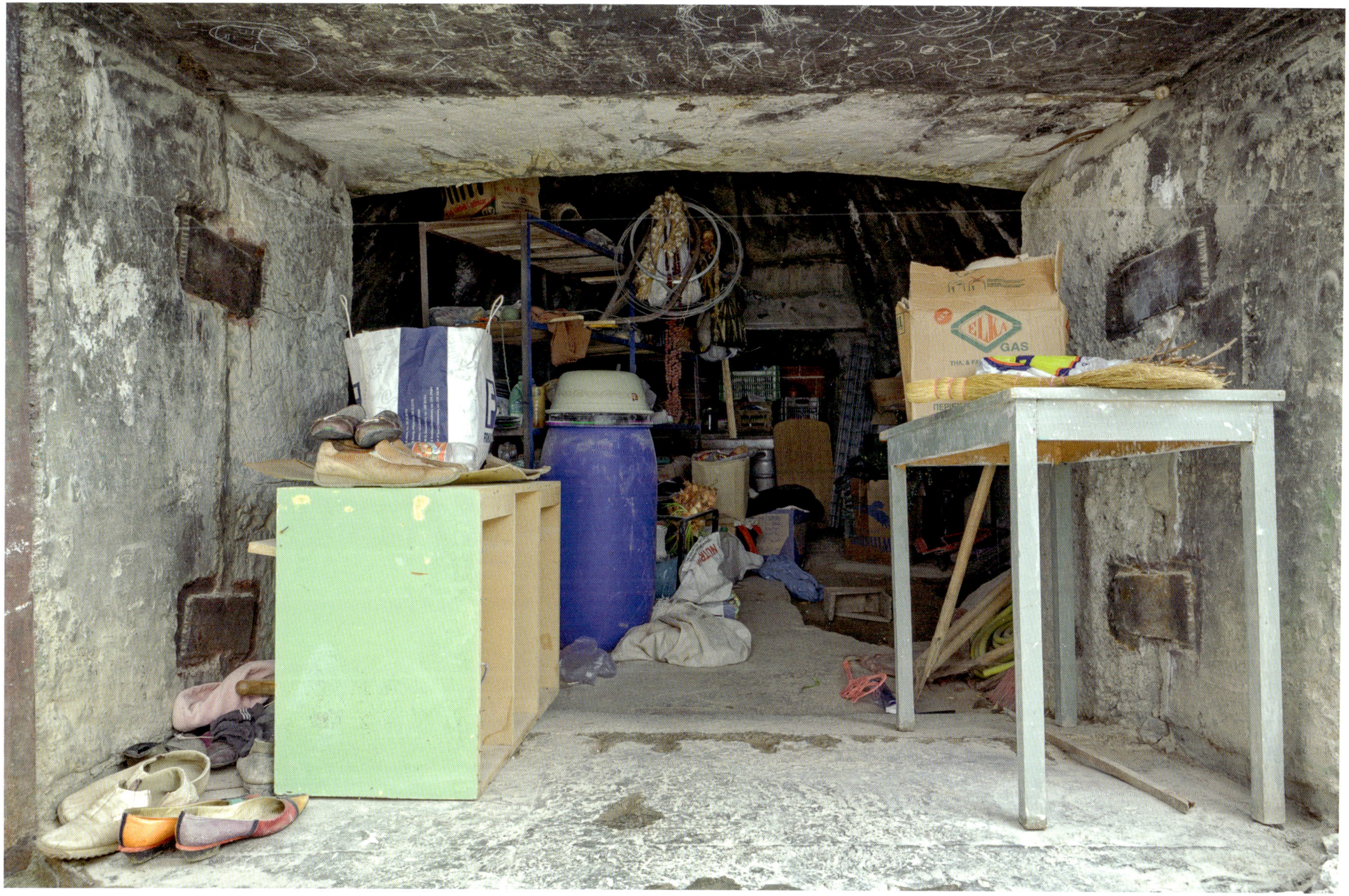
ELKA
GAS

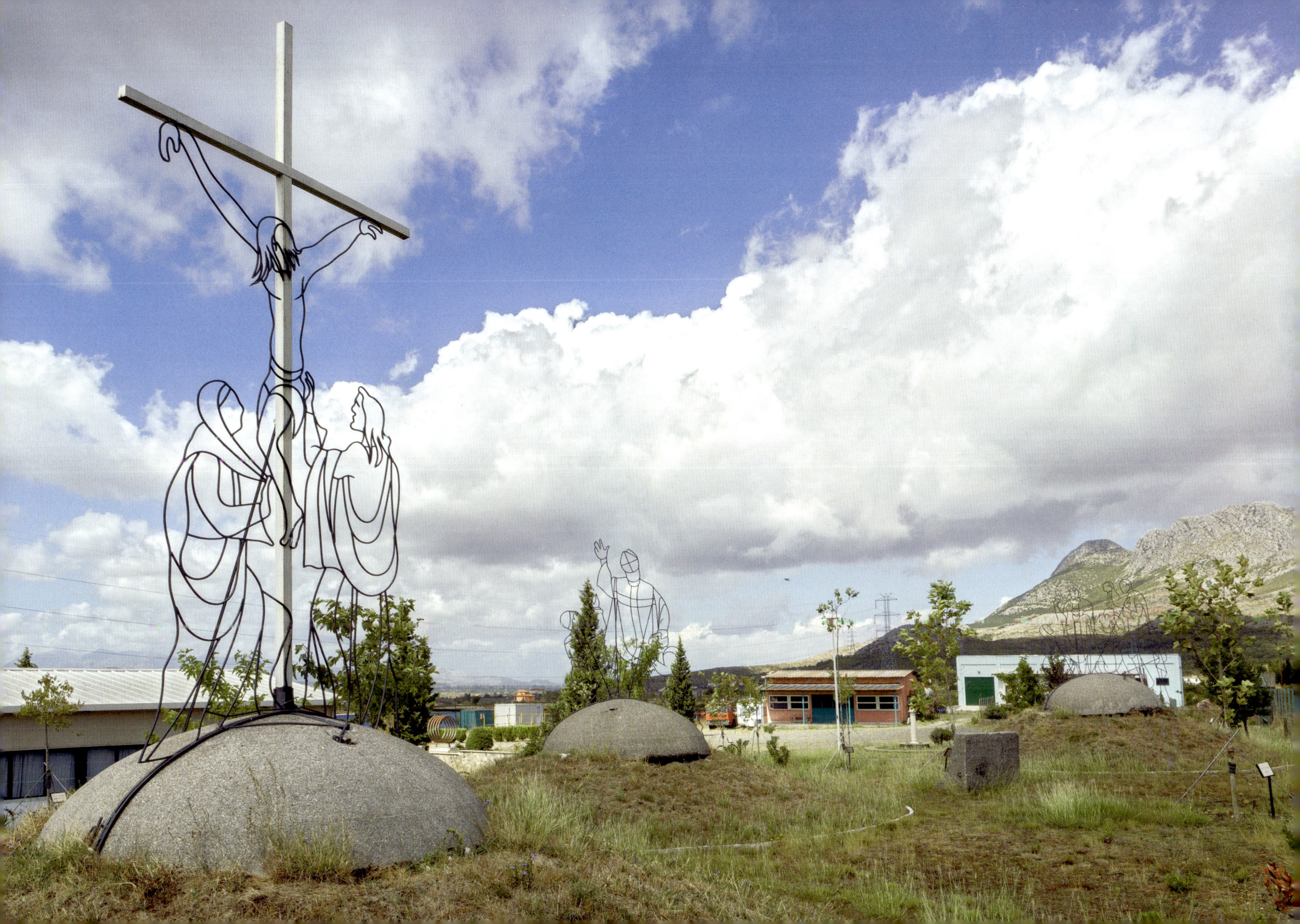

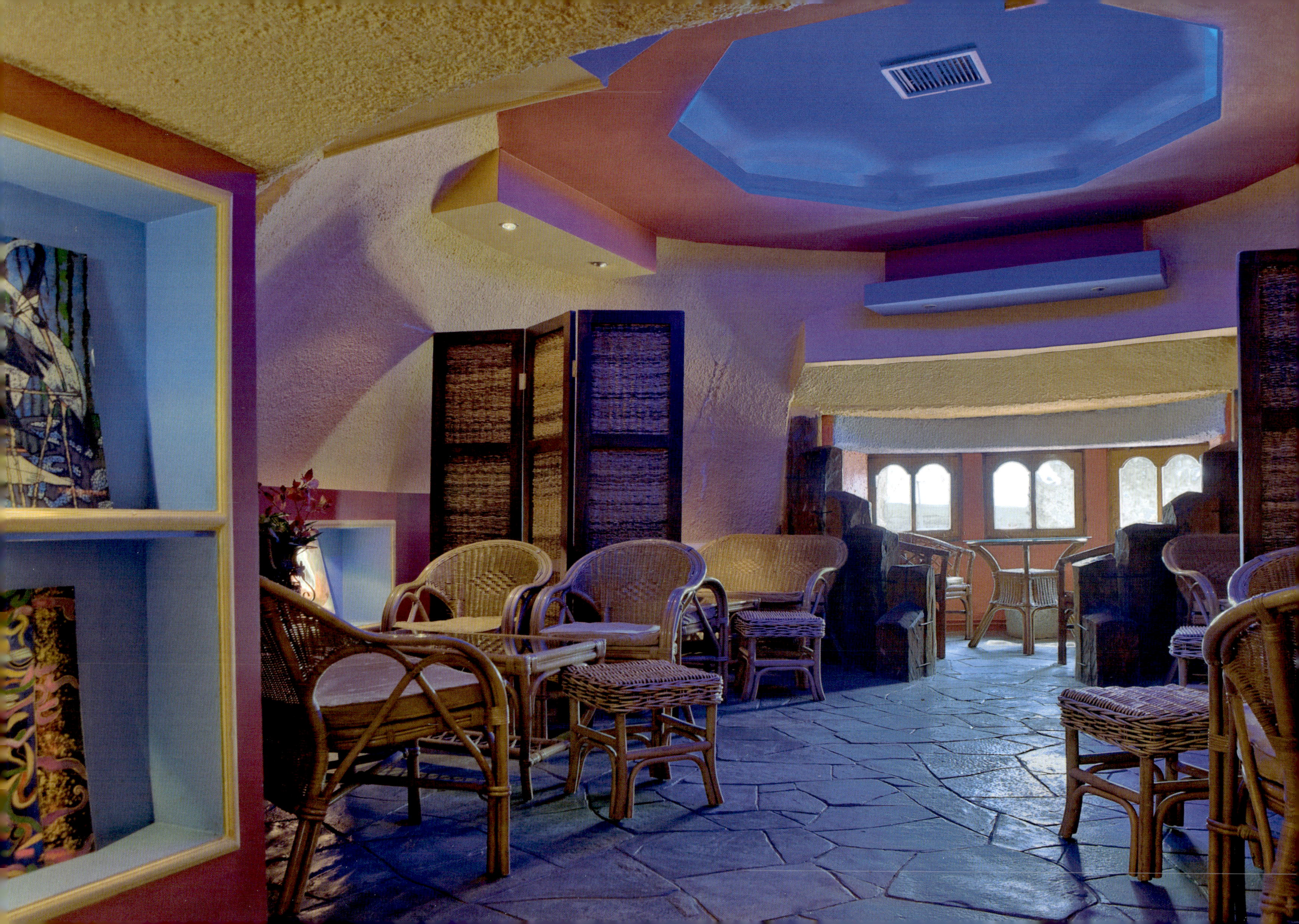

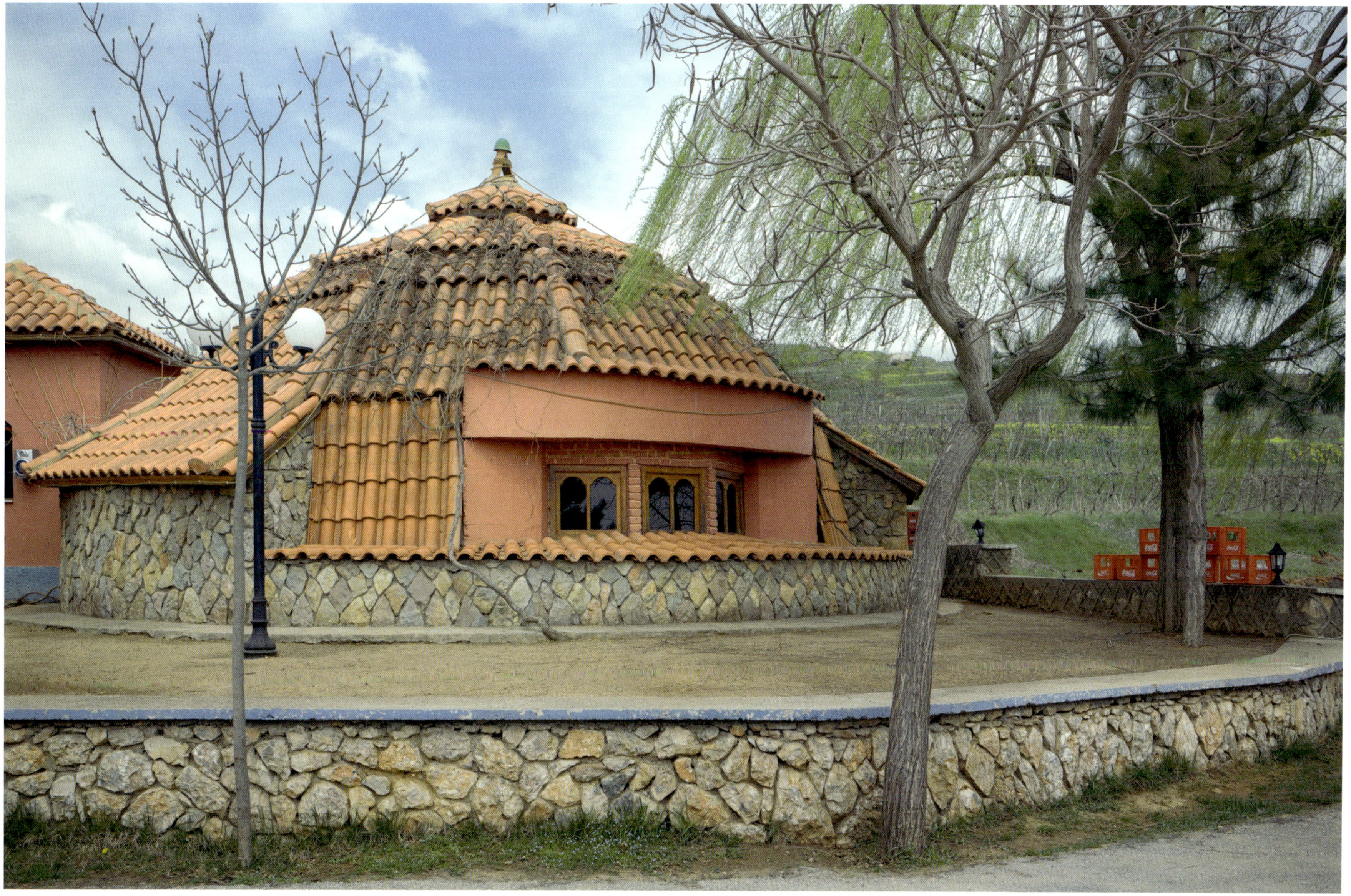

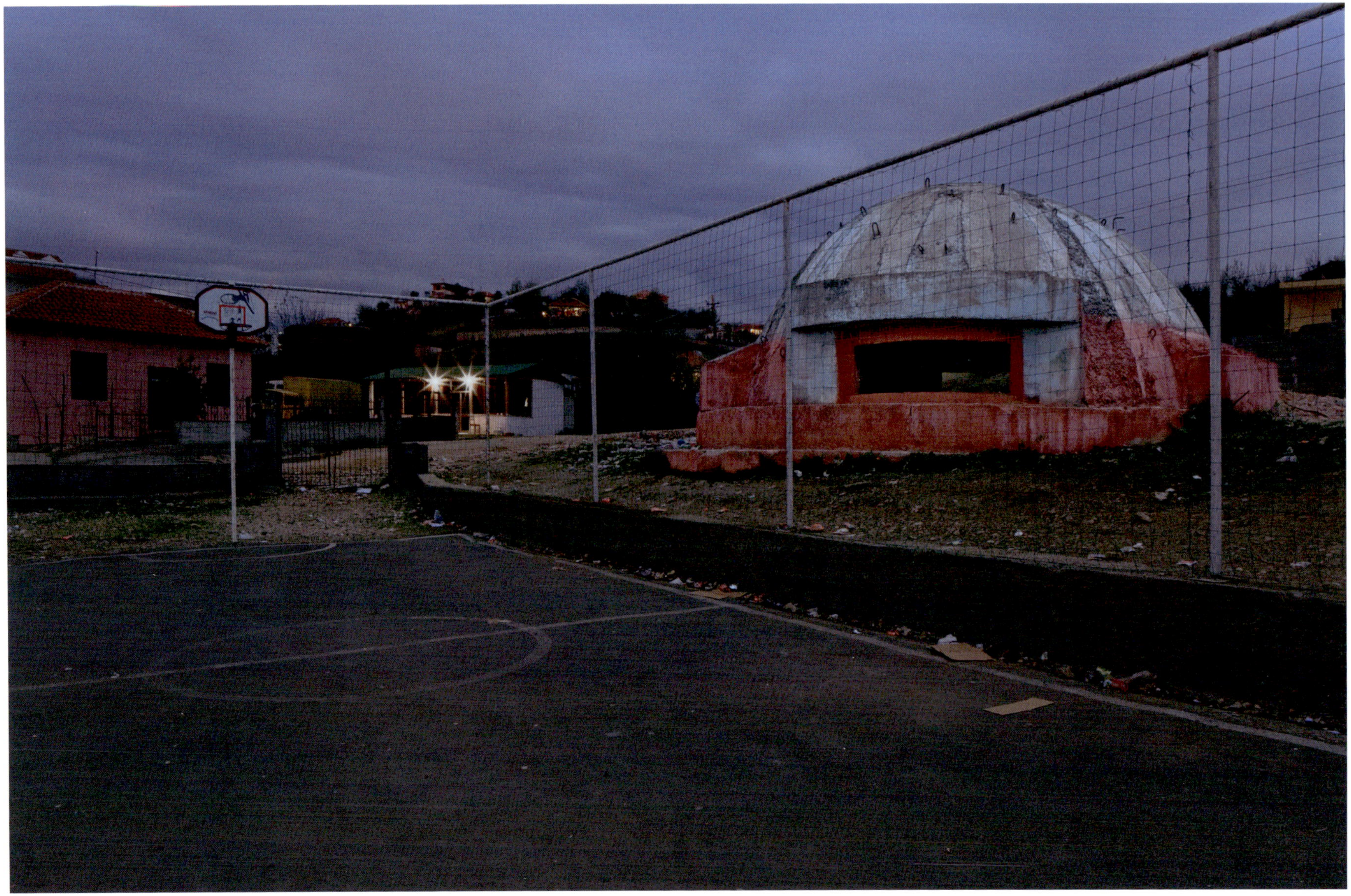

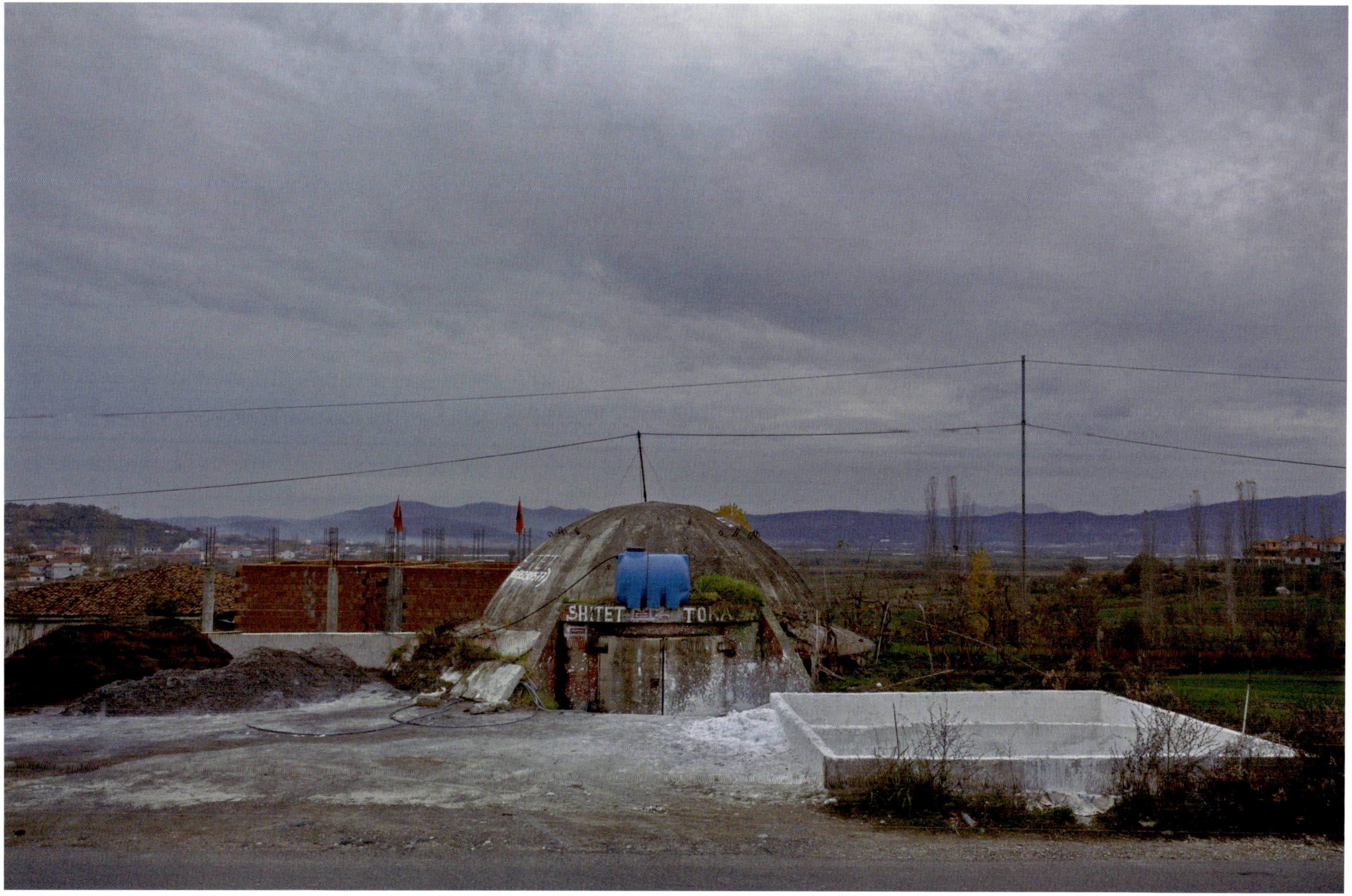
SHITET

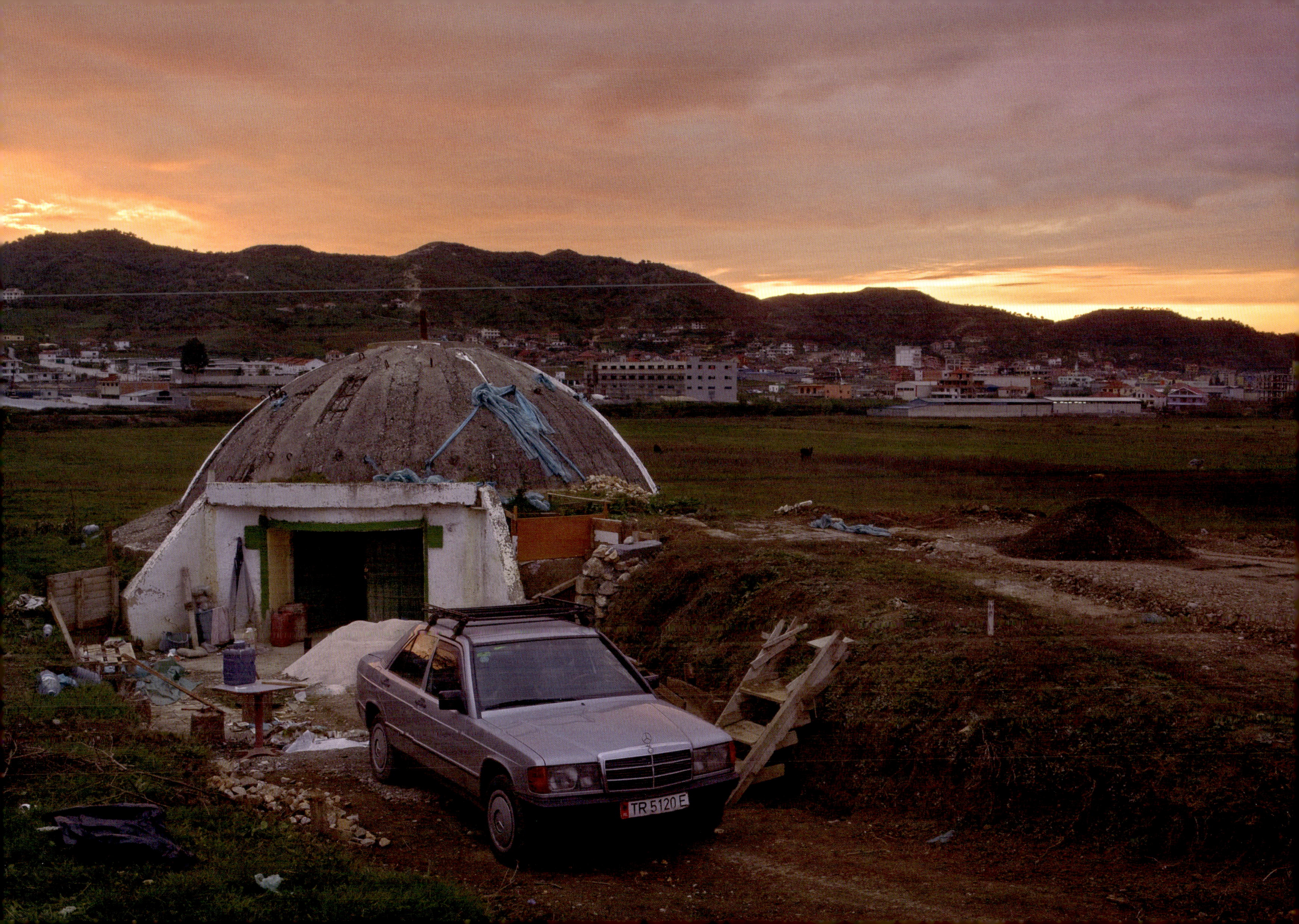
TR 5120 E

INTERVIEW WITH ALFRED MOISIU

Alfred Spiro Moisiu was born in 1929 in the northern Albania city of Shkodër. As the son of a national hero of the Second World War, Moisiu followed his father into the Albanian army and rose to the rank of general. Having studied military engineering with distinctions in St Petersburg and Moscow, he was assigned the task of fortifying Albania with defensive bunkers until his reassignment as commander of a military engineers' company in 1982.

He left active service in 1984 but with the fall of communism in 1991 he returned to public life as Minister of Defence. During the early 1990s he was instrumental in the preparations for Albania's NATO membership. Politically neutral, and with his diplomatic skills and experience in public service, he was seen as a fitting candidate for the Presidency of Albania, and was elected to the post in 2002 for a term of five years.

Moisiu is the author of numerous papers and books relating to defence and security.

Interviewed by Robert Hackman, 11th April 2009, Tirana, Albania.

RH: These bunkers could still be here in 1,000 years. We're not even a generation away from when they were built yet people don't know much about why and how they were built.

AM: People have viewed the construction of bunkers as related to communism and their construction has been used politically, internally and externally, to attack communism. But bunkers were built at a time the USA and the former Soviet Union spent $720 billion a year, some $2 billion a day, as part of their military budget. Albania could not afford to produce aeroplanes and missiles and so we built bunkers instead.

Albania's mad military and political strategy during the Cold War was: be ready to fight and confront NATO or the Warsaw Pact, and win. Of course, we could confront them but winning was another issue.

In order to build the network of bunkers, we studied all the military fortification lines of 20th century history: the Maginot Line that the French built during WWI, the Ziegfried Line built by the Germans, the Stalin Line built by the Russians and also the fortifications built by the Americans in Vietnam. The idea behind it was that our soldiers and ammunitions would be protected while in the battlefield, so they wouldn't come under direct fire. We studied the land near the sea and deep inside the country, including the land bordering Greece and the former Yugoslavia and we could say that Albania was fortified in all directions.

So we built bunkers to shelter soldiers and ammunitions while fighting, bigger bunkers to shelter heavy artillery, and tunnels from where military operations would be led. In addition there was an anti-aircraft defence line and ammunition depots built all over the country, the latter were built in such a way that if one exploded, it wouldn't affect the other depots.

RH: Are the bunkers a Chinese or Soviet model?

AM: Neither, they are an original Albanian model. We had a design institute employing over 100 technicians. We experimented on the ground hitting the bunkers with heavy artillery. The first experiments were in 1976 in Gryken e Kelcyres and Mezhgoranit and the second in 1977 in Palavi, Saranda. Animals, including dogs from the border patrol as they were well trained and therefore more intelligent, were placed inside the bunkers to see the effect of heavy artillery on them. After the bombardment the dogs were a bit confused but came back to shape quickly. The best doctors at the time were engaged to observe the effects on the animals.

RH: When did bunker construction start and end?

AM: Bunkers were built during different periods. Some during King Zog's reign (Prime Minister 1922-1924, King 1925-1939). A few between 1948 and 1949 in various areas. The communist bunkers were built from January 1975 until 1982 when I was deputy Minister of Defence. I was then dismissed, but construction continued until about 1986. So the construction of bunkers lasted for about 10 or more years. Many bunkers were built, but not as many as the exaggerated numbers reported by the media or the figures quoted on various websites. There was a specific and accurate inventory system and it's with the Army's General Staff. I can't remember the exact number because construction continued after I was dismissed, however there is an exact number in the army archives.

RH: A few of the bunkers I have photographed have been dated 1988.

AM: Maybe they were built after 1986, I don't know.

RH: What's your guess on the number of bunkers?

AM: I don't know. Maybe 500,000.

RH: Is it true that building bunkers consumed the GDP for four years?

AM: It's difficult to say because there were various expenses. Cement was produced in the country, iron was partly produced in Albania and partly imported free of charge from China. Builders/workers came both from the army and the people. Transport was another cost. There were huge expenses and costs involved in the bunkerfication of Albania. It would have been a different story if these materials and labour had been used for the construction of roads and other civilian projects. However, all the world was crazy back then.

RH: So the only material imported was the metal used in the concrete reinforcement?

AM: Yes.

RH: When was the most prevalent design of the communist bunkers that we see today conceived?

AM: In 1975.

RH: Was there any consideration to use the Chinese design of an underground network of tunnels?

AM: The Albanian model was influenced by the design of the Siegfried Line in Germany, but with a far greater quantity of bunkers. The Parimi (factories) – the prefabrication and later installation – was modelled on the Americans' approach in Vietnam. The bunkers' cover or roof was initially made from two pieces but after testing it didn't prove to be very solid, and so it was later built as one piece. The base was made of two pieces. The part that linked the bunker with the ground/underground was of special material and mounted with heavy machinery. These were produced in the industrial production factories, transported by huge trucks, deposited in main centres and then transported in military trucks to the designated site where the bunker would be assembled. The trucks were either produced in the country or imported. The first trucks were imported from Japan.

RH: What was the plan for assembling bunkers in specific areas?

AM: There was detailed planning of the production, transport and assembly of the bunkers. There were special groups of military soldiers to assemble the bunker parts. Each had a construction technician assigned to them. It was a perfect organisation, a huge job that even I who was involved cannot imagine how we achieved it. If all that human energy, not just the materials, had been put to other uses, I can't imagine where Albania would be today.

Construction of the bunker parts took place in construction companies where people worked in shifts. There was a strict quality control. There were two types of quality controllers – production quality and assembly quality. The latter control ensured that the bunkers were assembled in places that would be of benefit to the soldiers, sheltering them in the event of war.

RH: How many people were employed in the bunkerfication process?

AM: Numerous construction companies were employed. Each had a work schedule of three shifts per day. Each shift had its own construction programme. As for the assembly of the bunker parts, Luan Hoxha (a senior army officer) was appointed as the officer responsible.

RH: Were you supervising production and assembly of the bunkers?

AM: Everything. From the quality of cement and iron through to assembly.

RH: Today many people attempt to remove or modify bunkers, and they always comment on how tough the concrete is. Was anything done to make it extra tough?

AM: The high grade concrete can withstand pressure of 400 kg per cm^2. This concrete was produced because its strength increases as it matures over the years. They become more like castles as time passes. But unlike castles, which eventually crumble with time, bunkers only get tougher.

RH: How many construction factories were employed?

AM: Almost every city had one factory. For example there was one in the Saranda area in Toq. In Elbasan there were two places, in Tirana it was the Rruga Ura enterprise, and in Lac, Gjirokastër.

RH: How was the distribution of bunkers decided?

AM: Studies were made by the General Military Staff. By analysing the terrain and geography they would make theoretical battle assimilations and accordingly decide the best locations. It wasn't a random process. Bunkers were constructed where fighting was expected. All bunkers had open windows. Each defence group, consisting of ten soldiers, had about 7 to 9 bunkers assigned to them. Each soldier was sheltered in a bunker with no soldier left in the open. One bunker per soldier.

RH: Were the larger bunkers used for sheltering artillery?

AM: Yes, each artillery piece and tank had its own bunker and was supported by 4 to 7 soldiers depending on the size of the artillery.

RH: Were these bunkers continually inhabited?

AM: Soldiers were despatched to man the bunkers only in the event of possible hostility. The exception was the bunkers at border points which were manned continually. Whilst I was in the army there were 72,000 – 80,000 serving personnel. The Albanian army had at this time 1,200 tanks. During this period the former Yugoslavian army, which was the strongest in the Balkans had 1,500 tanks. Albania was a big military power in the region then and planned only for defence. There were also contingency plans for Kosovo and groups that could serve Albania in case events escalated.

RH: The years when bunkers were built also coincide with the years that Albania suspended its relations with its last ally The Peoples Republic of China. Did this breaking of diplomatic ties influence the magnitude of the bunkerfication project ?

AM: Of course, when relations were severed with the USSR in 1961 we started building bunkers, but a different type and not in large numbers. They were big and not of the same quality. In 1977 Albania broke with the Chinese and it was then that full-on construction commenced. Interestingly, in 1999 during the Kosovo war, all the bunkers along the northern border were ready to use in case the Yugoslavs attacked and came into Albania in an attempt to drag Albania into the conflict.

RH: Was there a difference between the party's policy of building bunkers and Enver Hoxha's?

AM: Enver Hoxha was the party. Even today it goes like that.

RH: How do you feel today seeing bunkers you helped build now used for other purposes?

AM: Bunkers were the choice, a solution during that period of the Cold War. It's similar to the American's missiles which have been dismantled or are now in museums, time goes by and you throw them away like old clothes. Everything has its time.

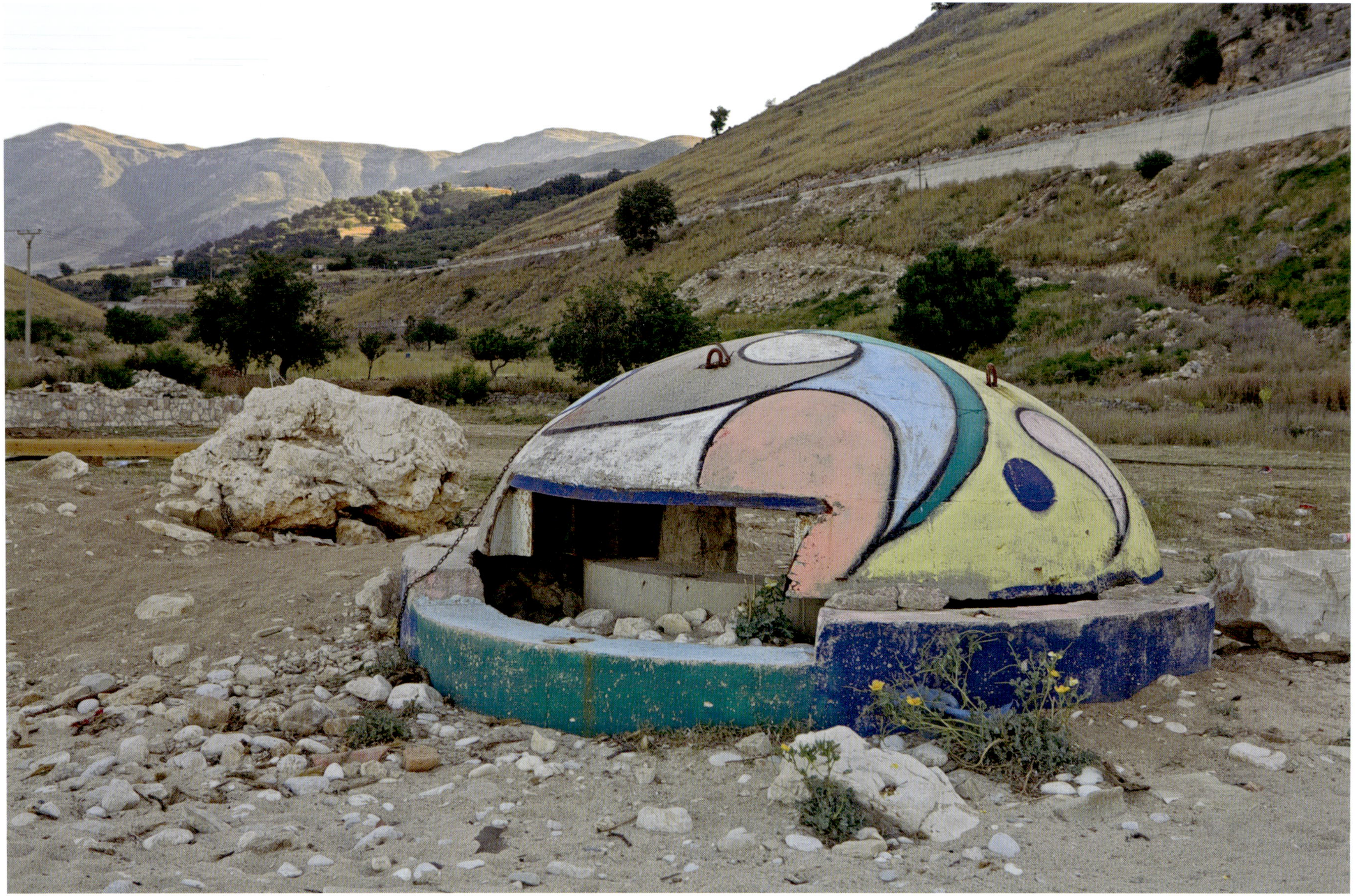

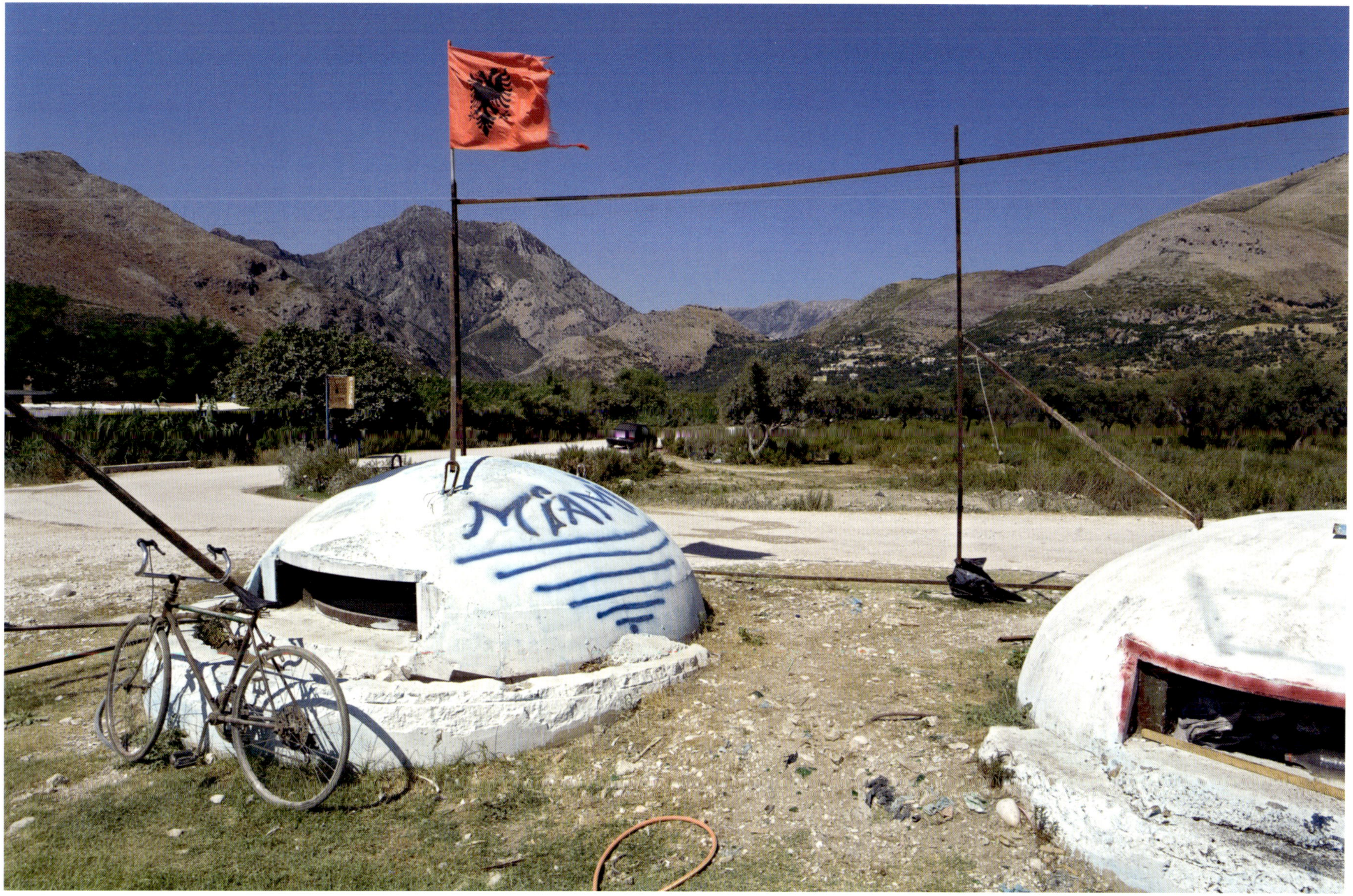

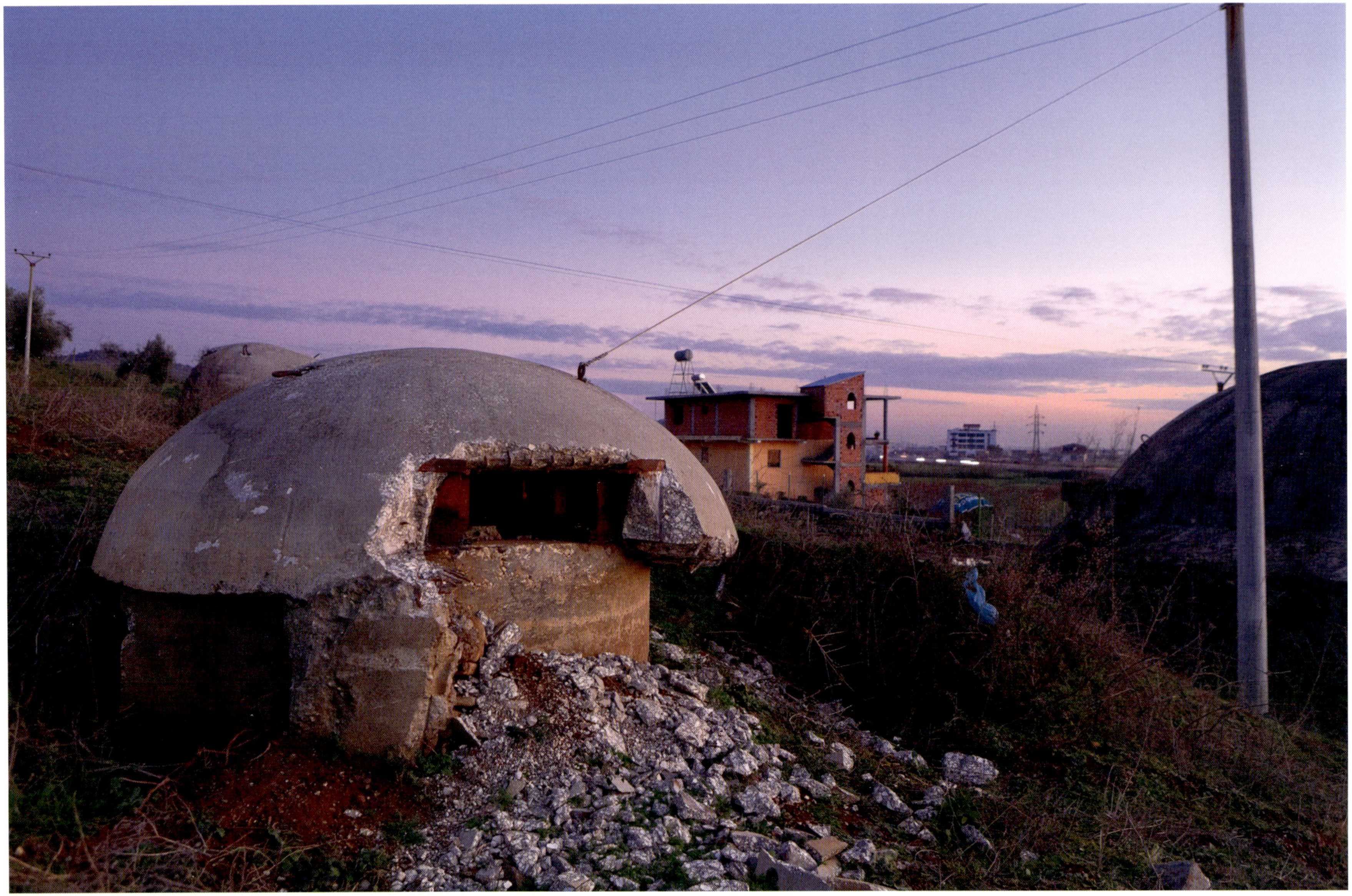

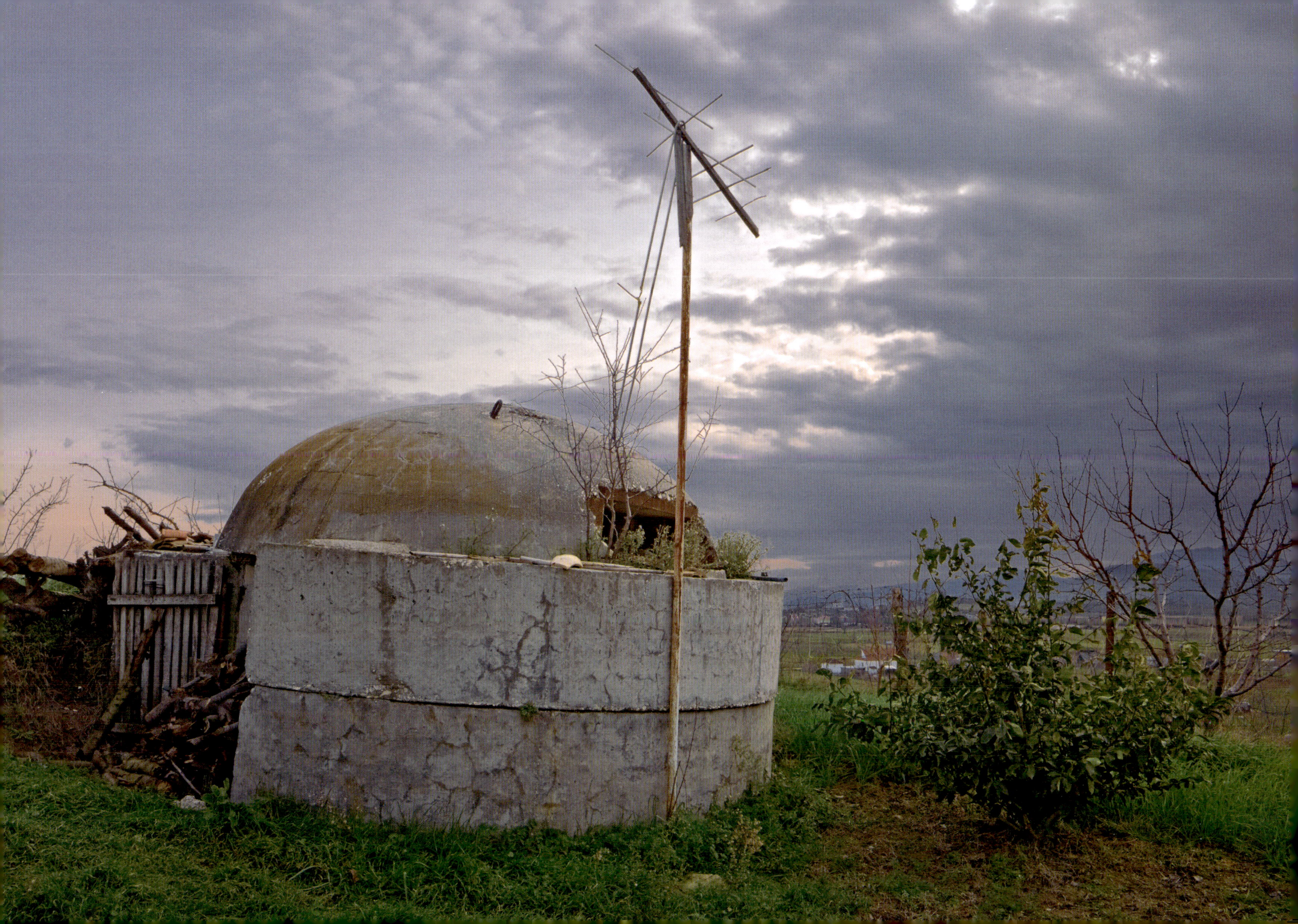

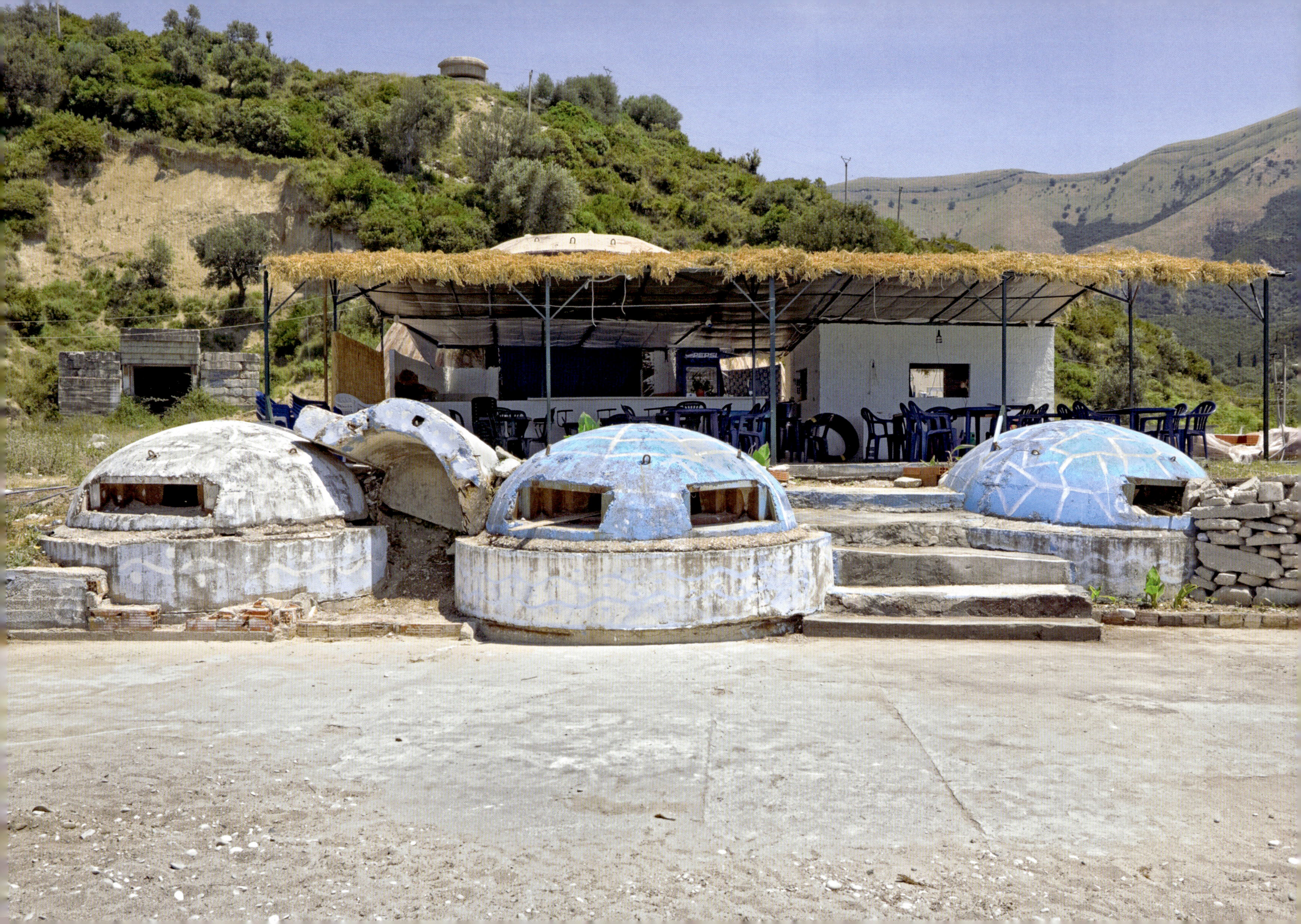

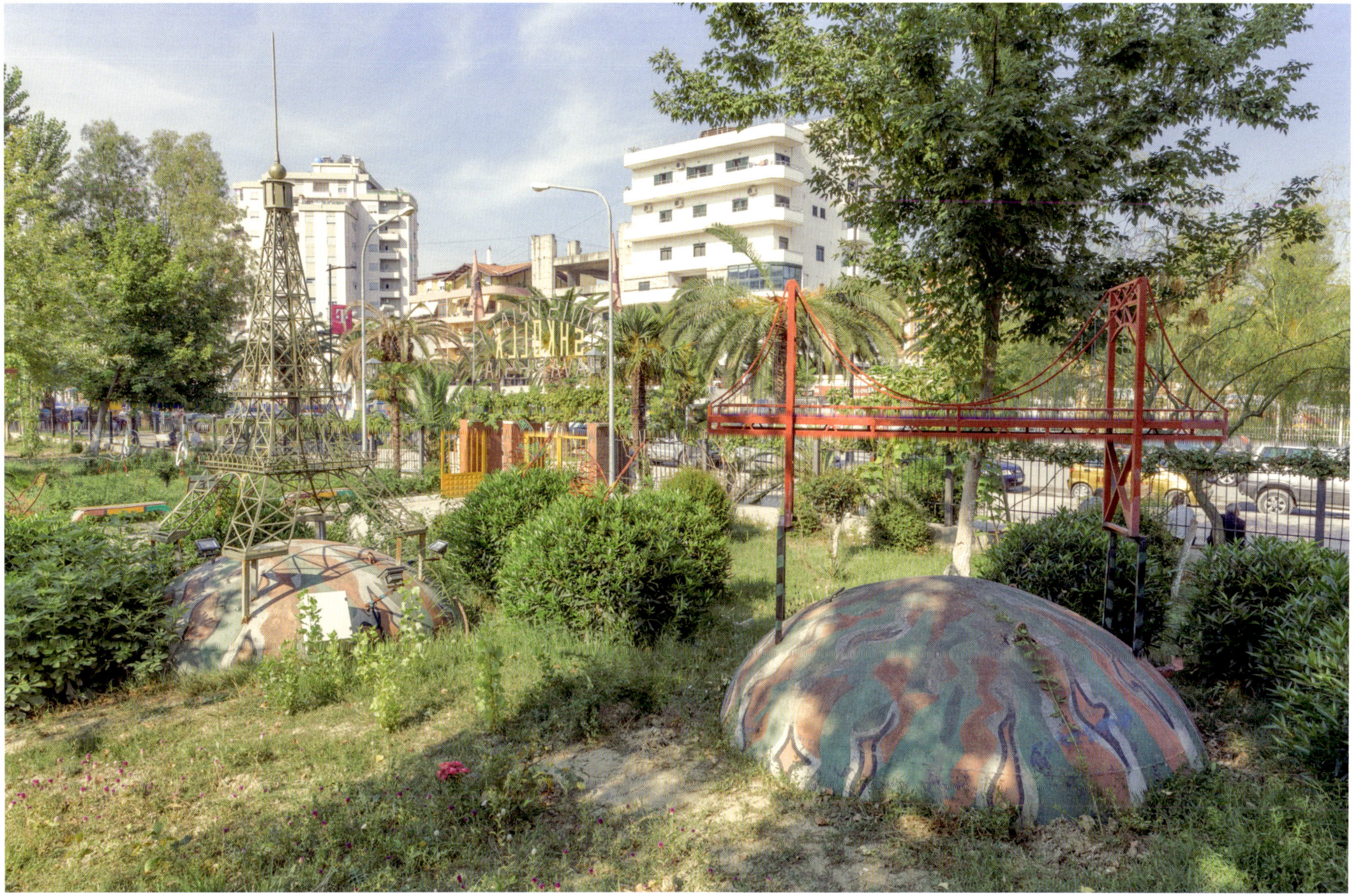

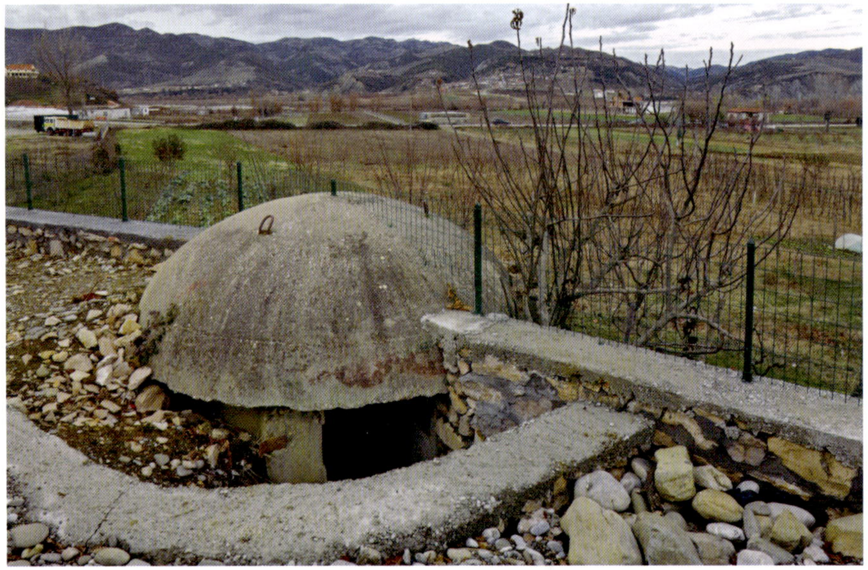

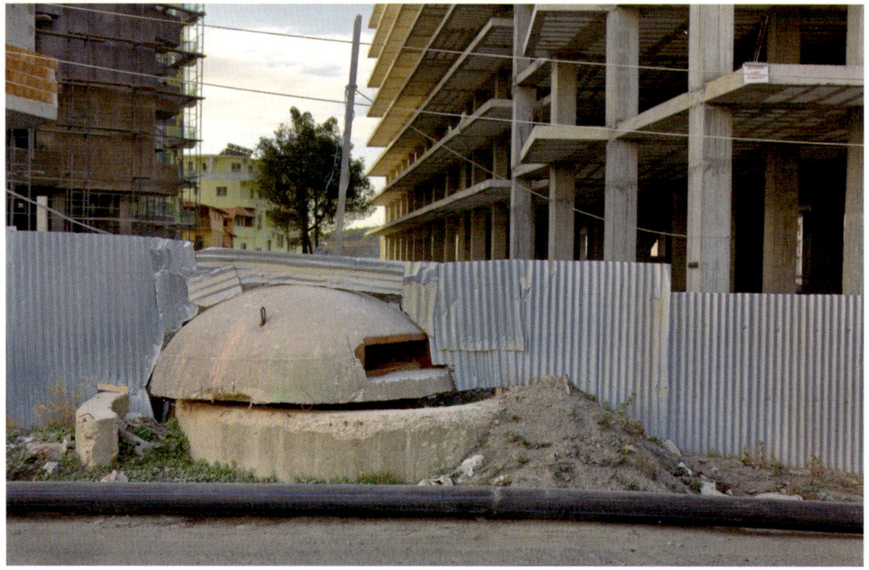

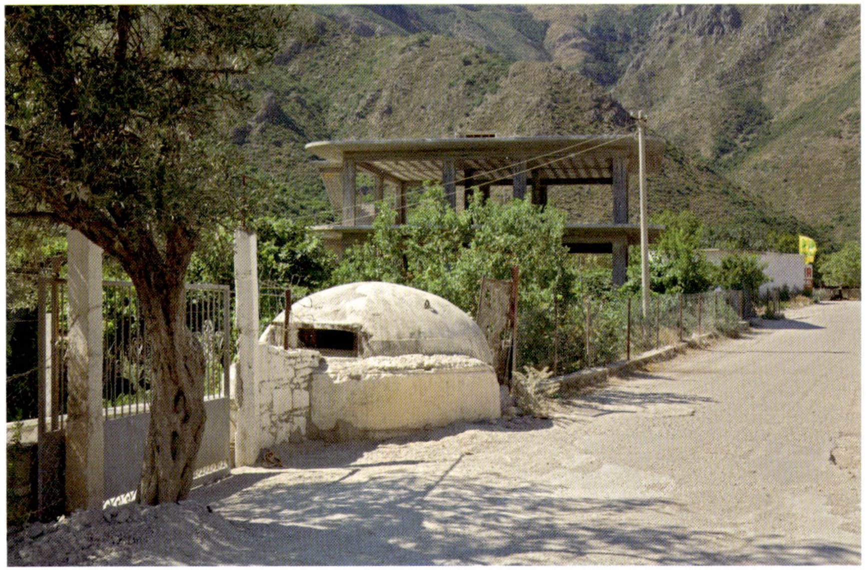

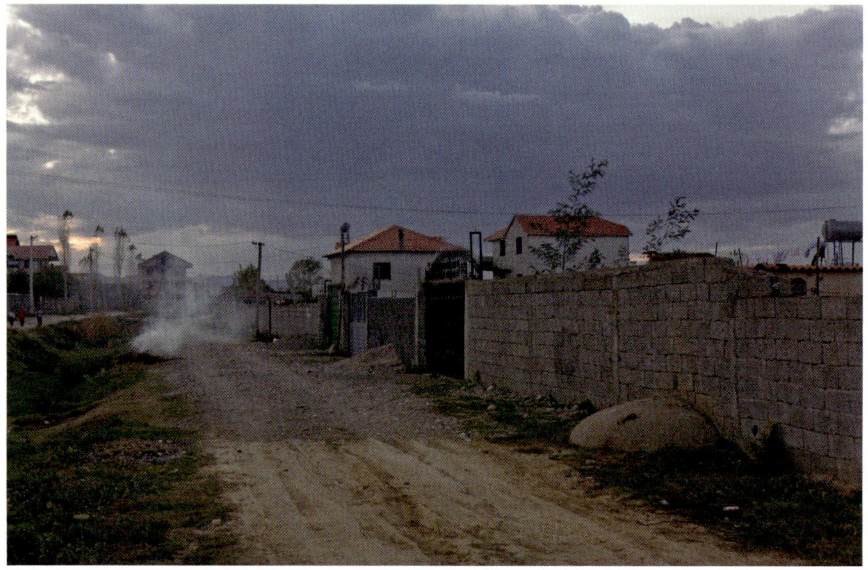

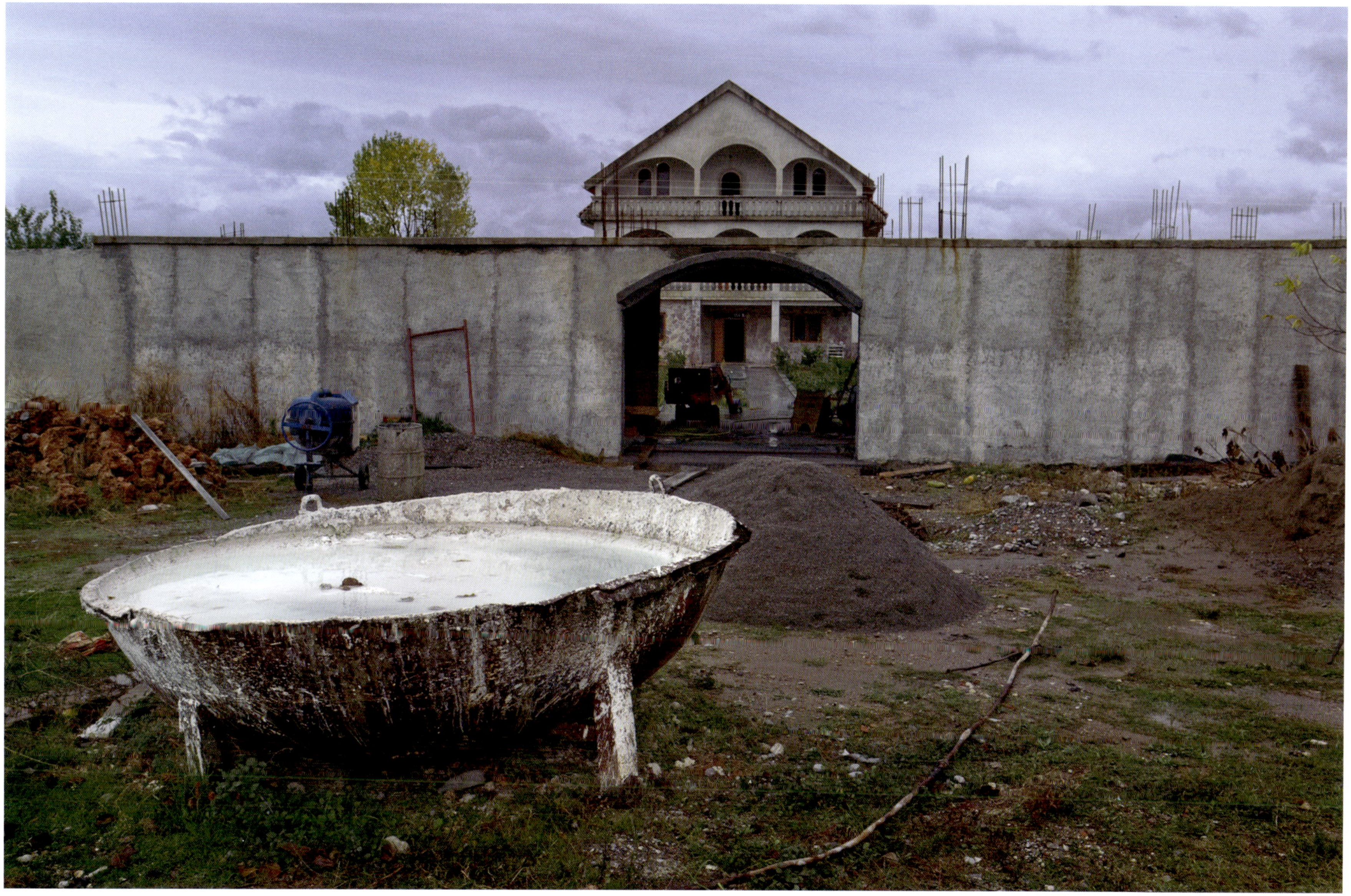

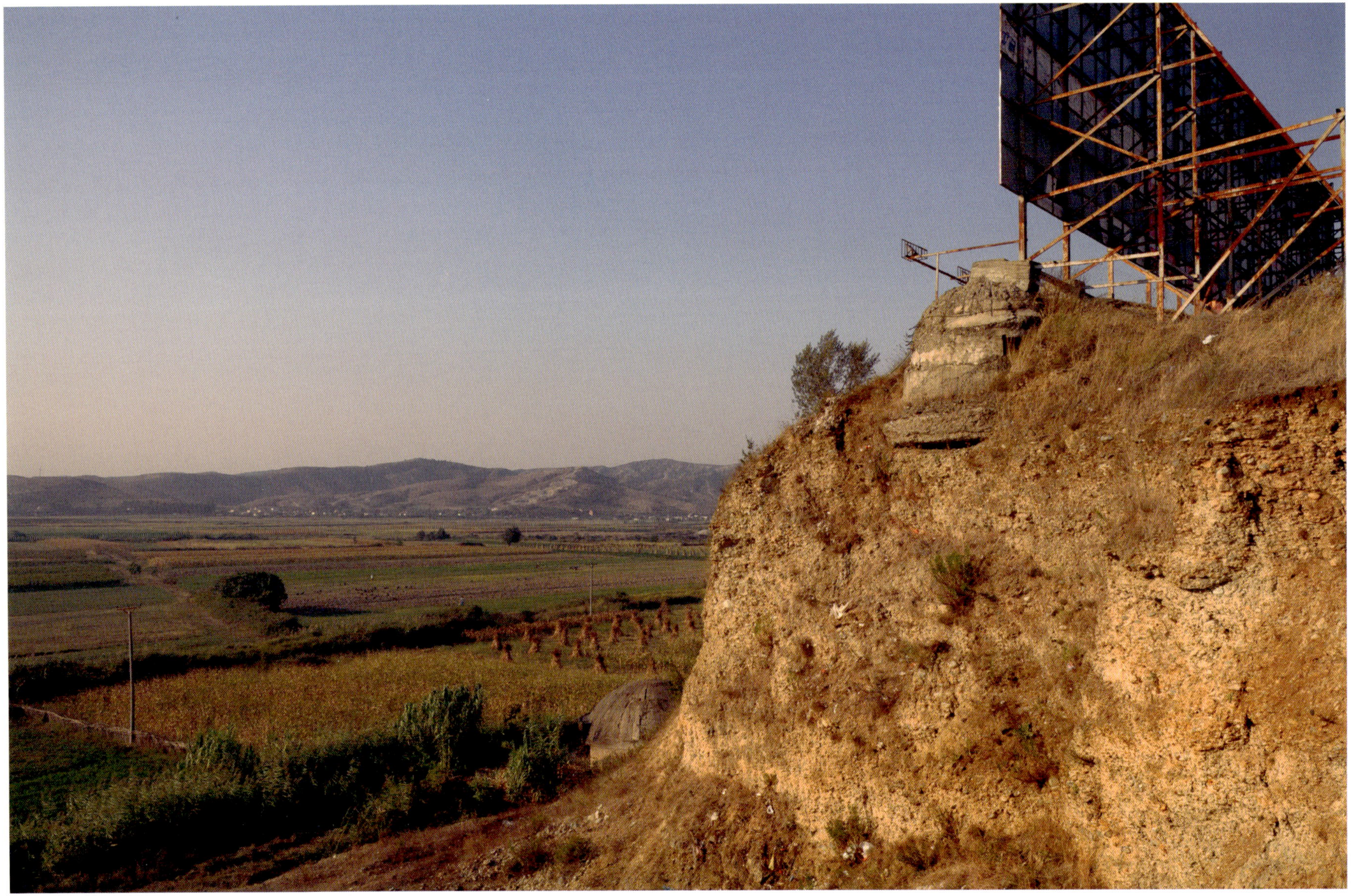

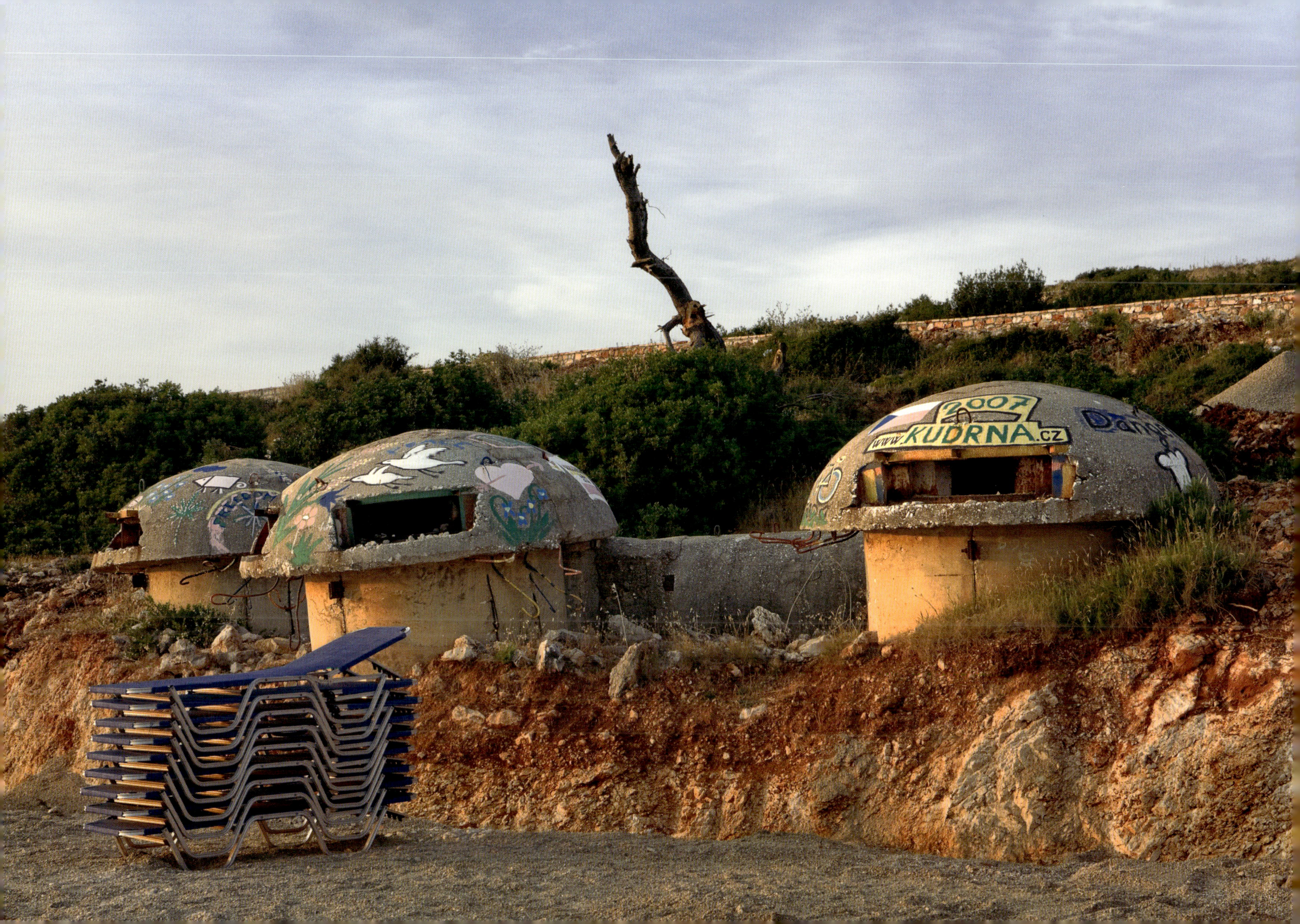
2007
www.KUDRNA.cz

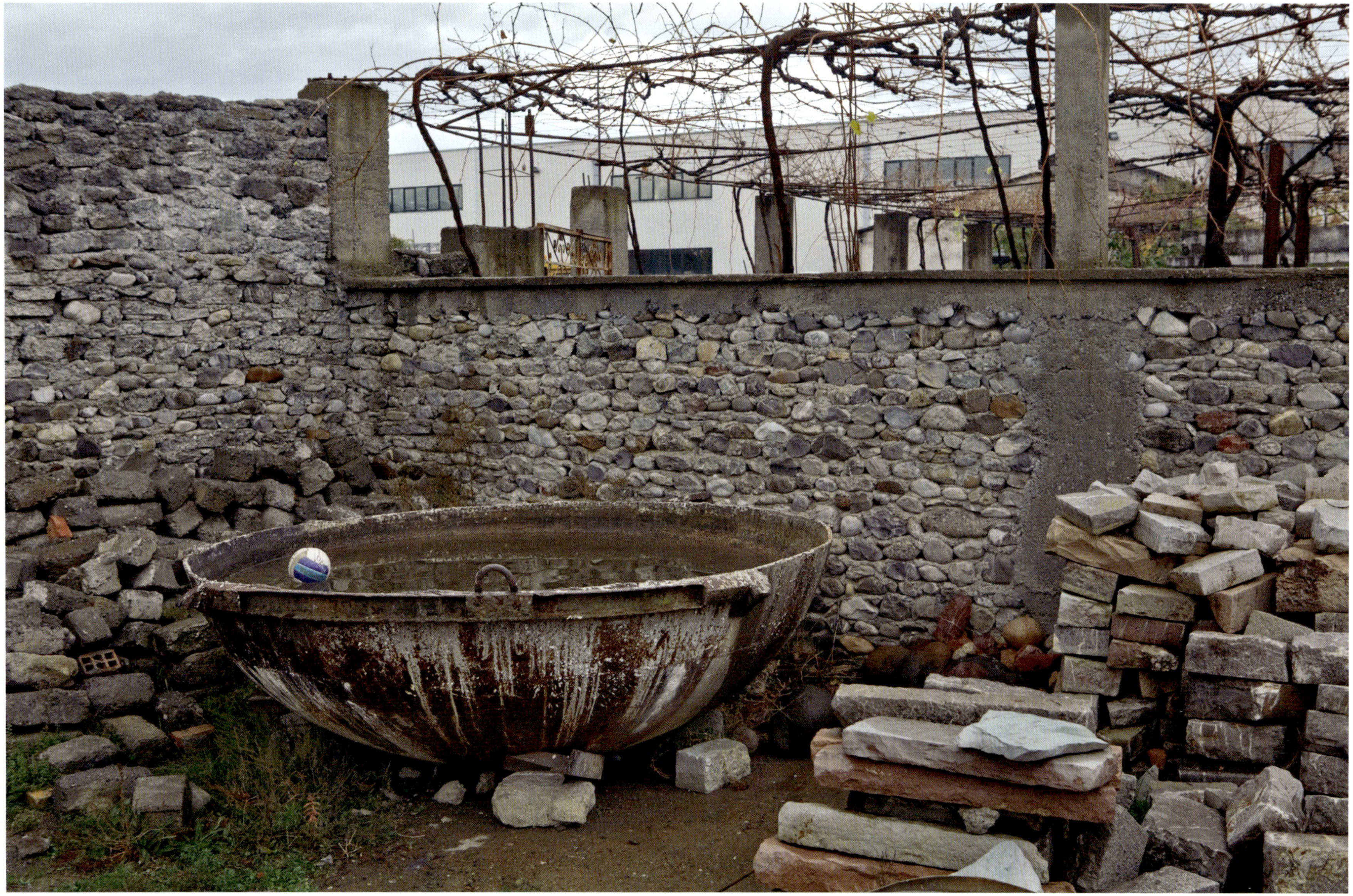

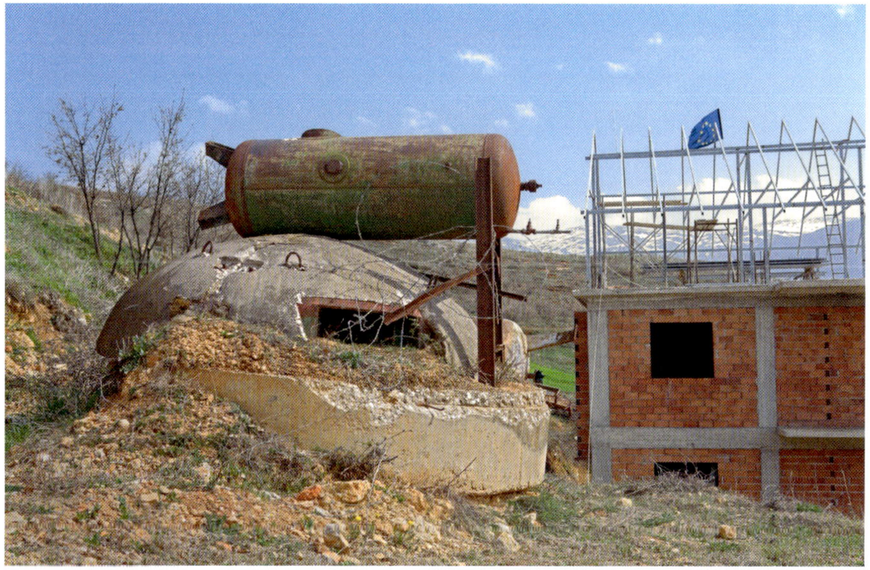

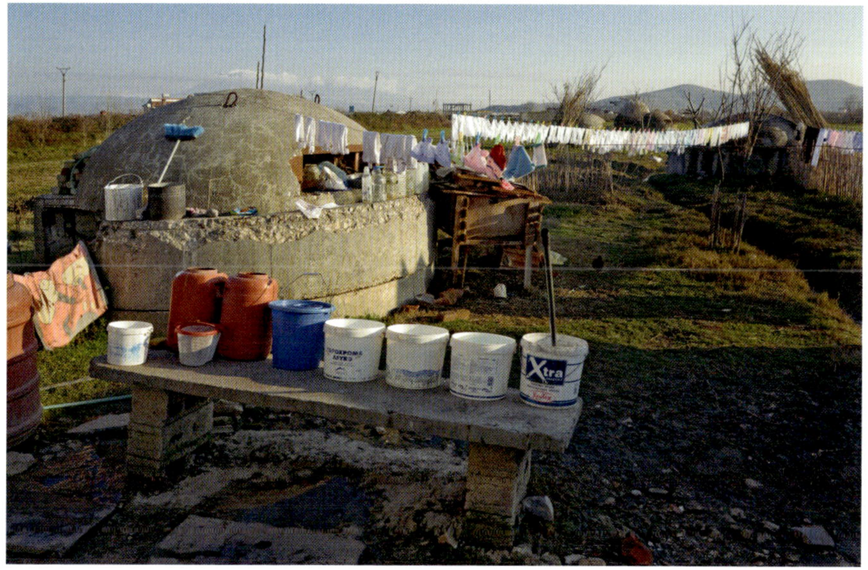
Xtra

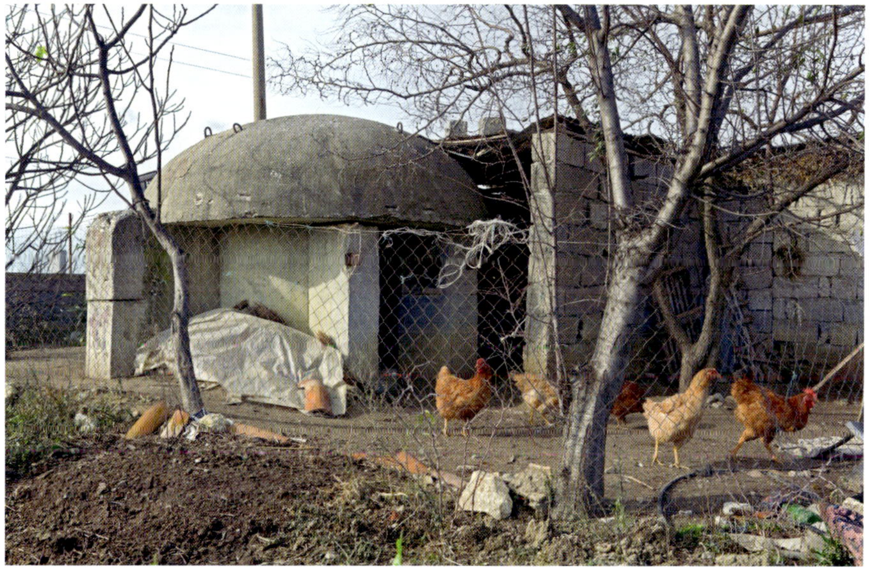

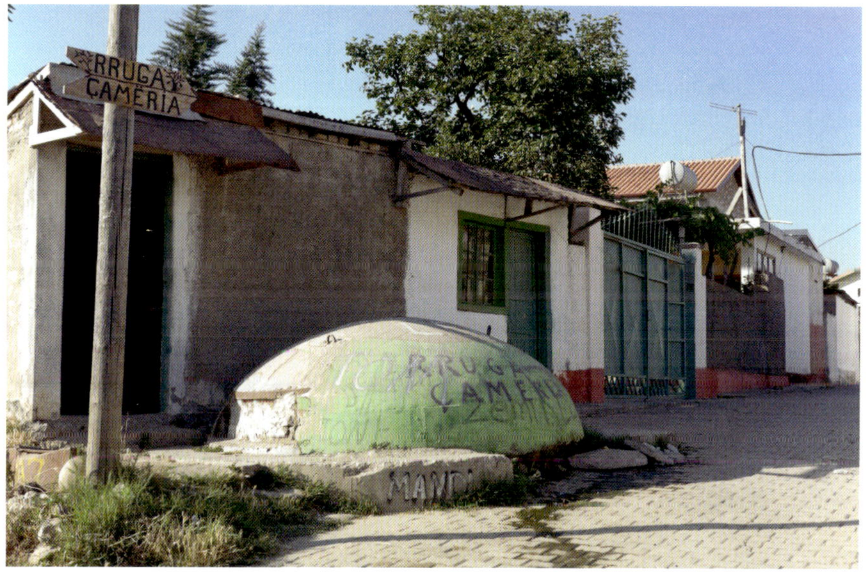
RRUGA
ÇAMERIA

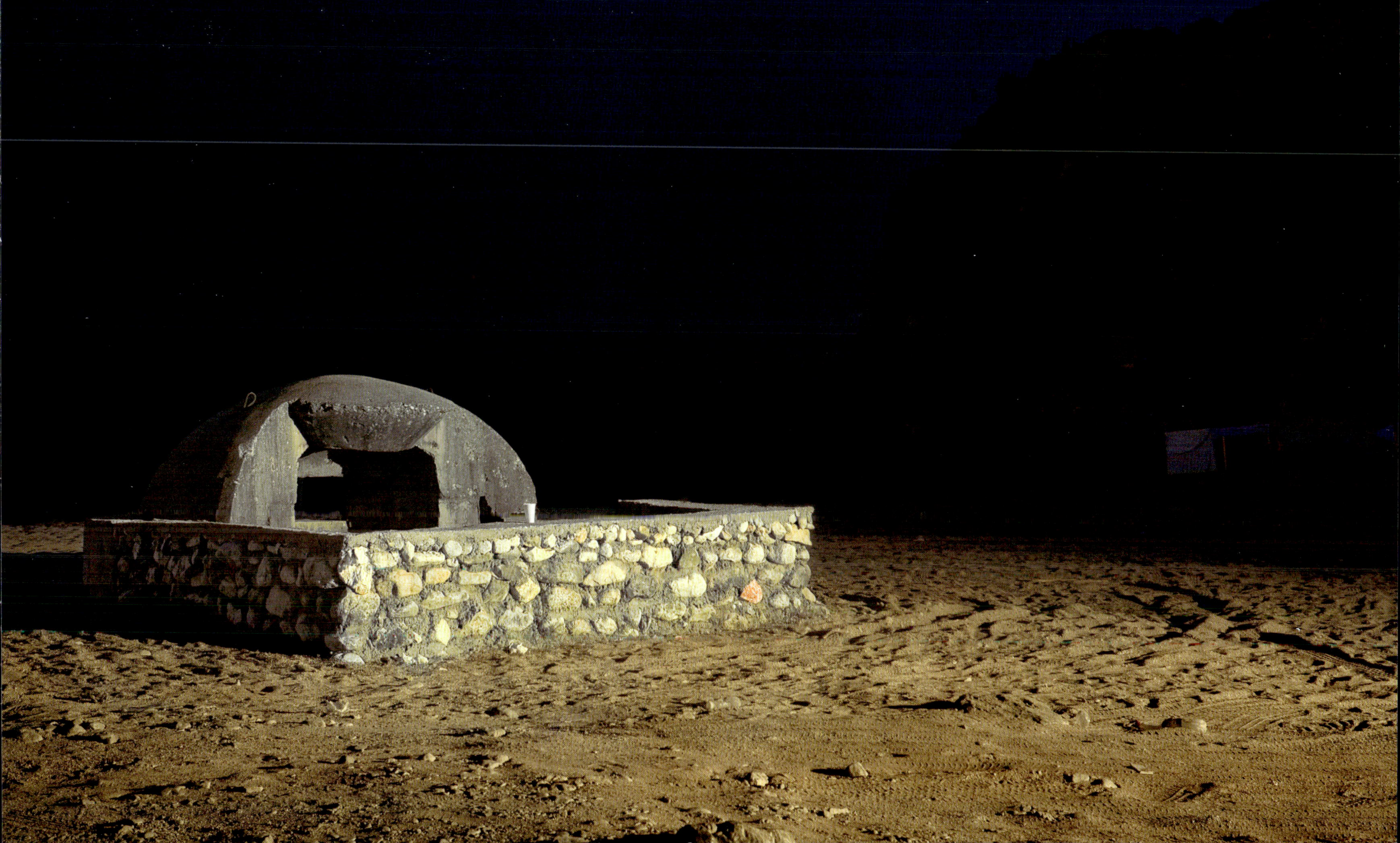

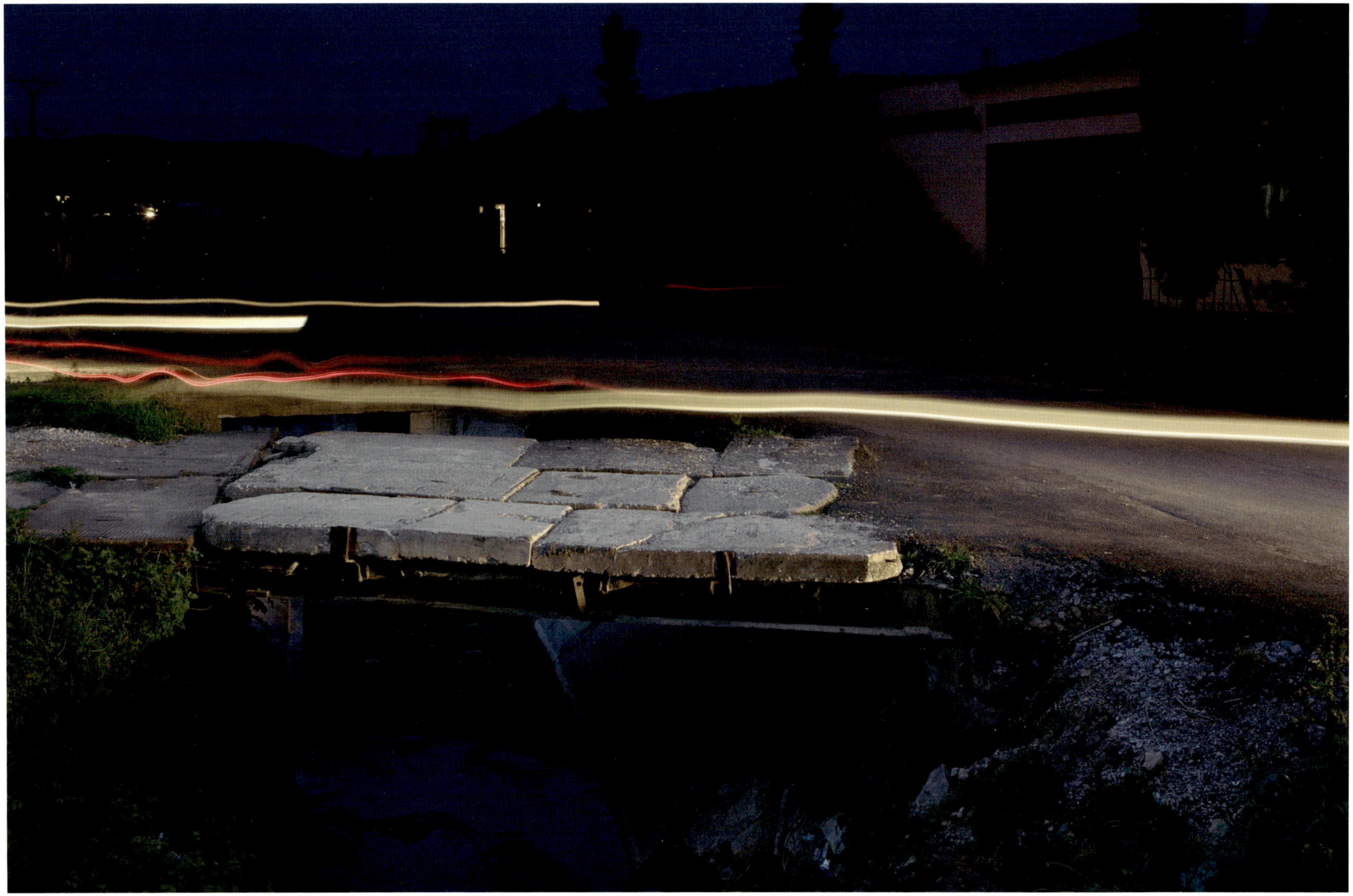

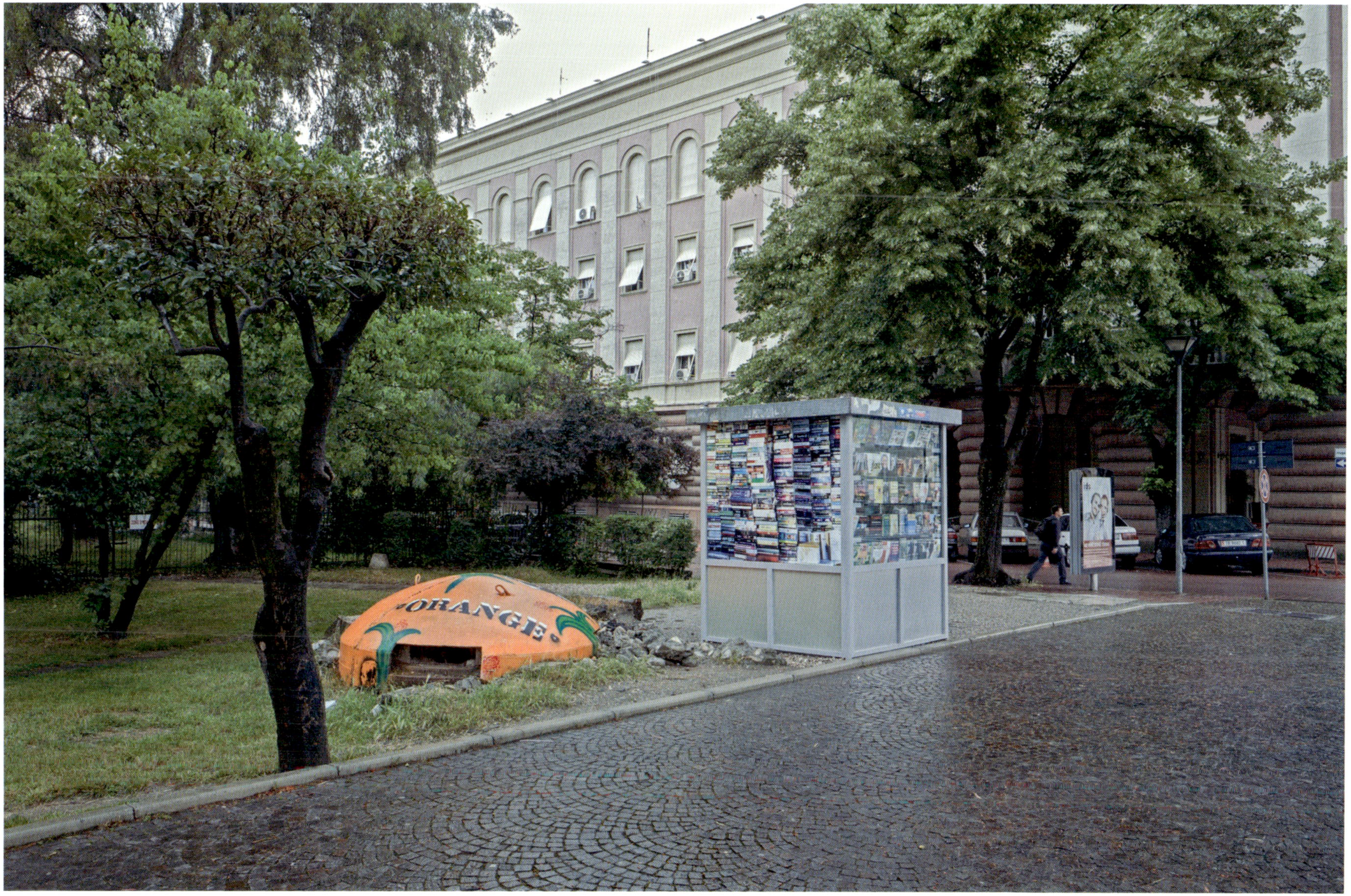
ORANGE

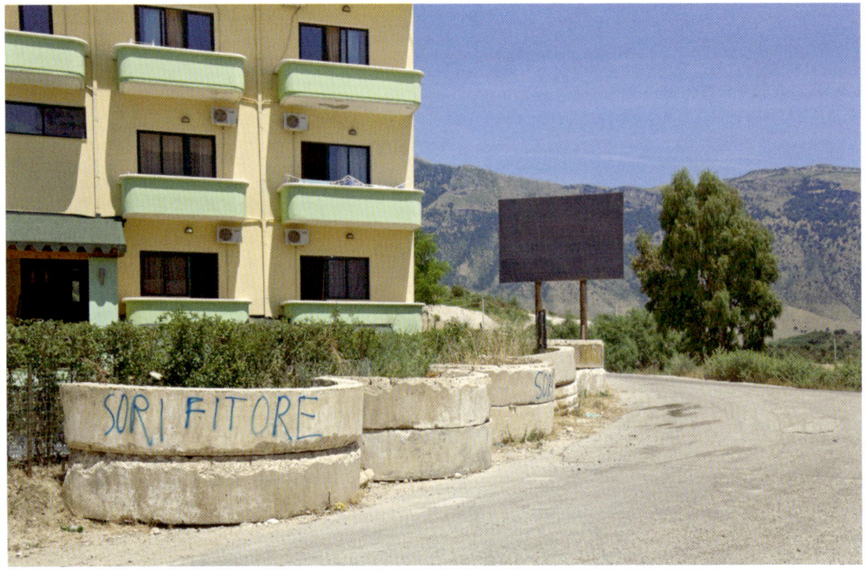
SORI FITORE

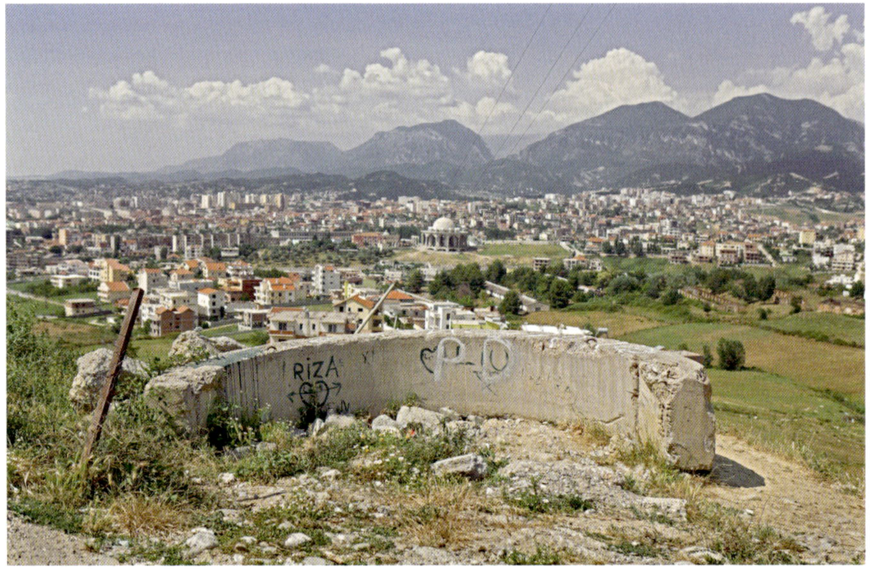
RIZA

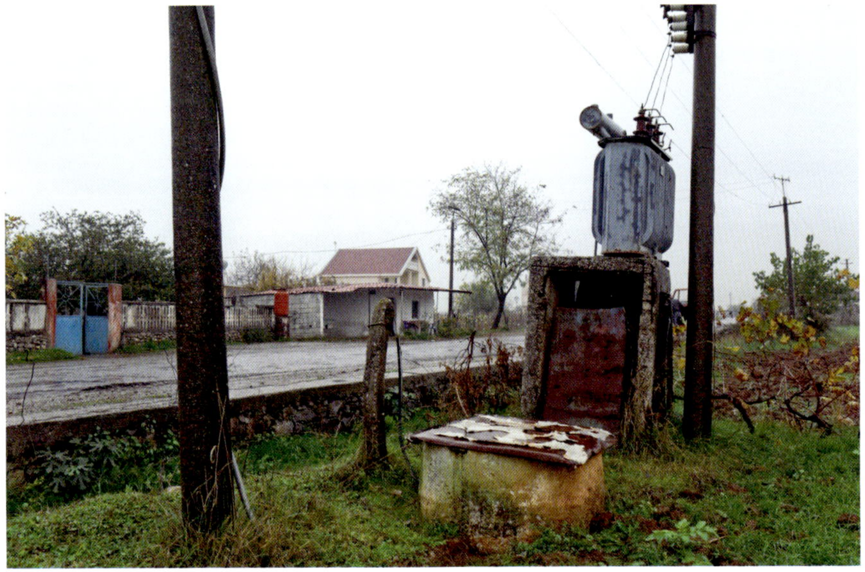

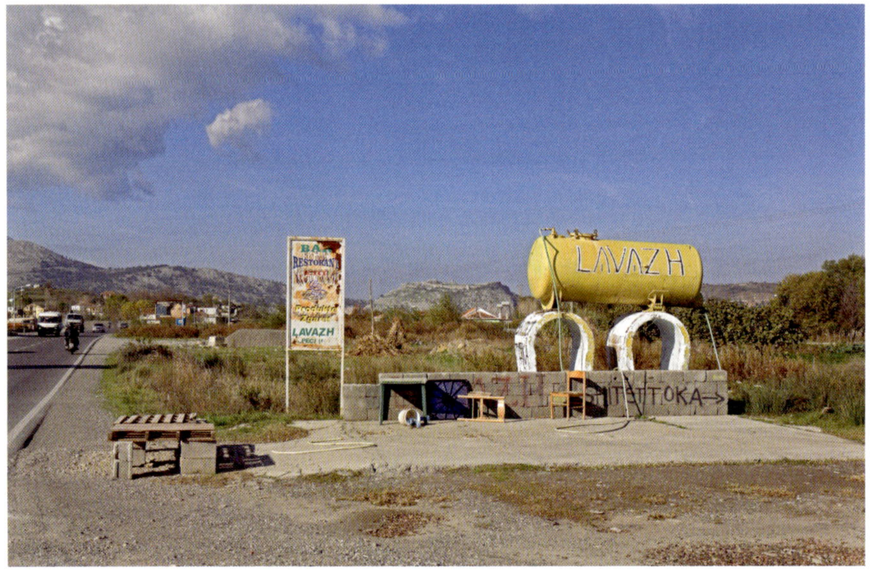
LAVAZH
LAVAZH

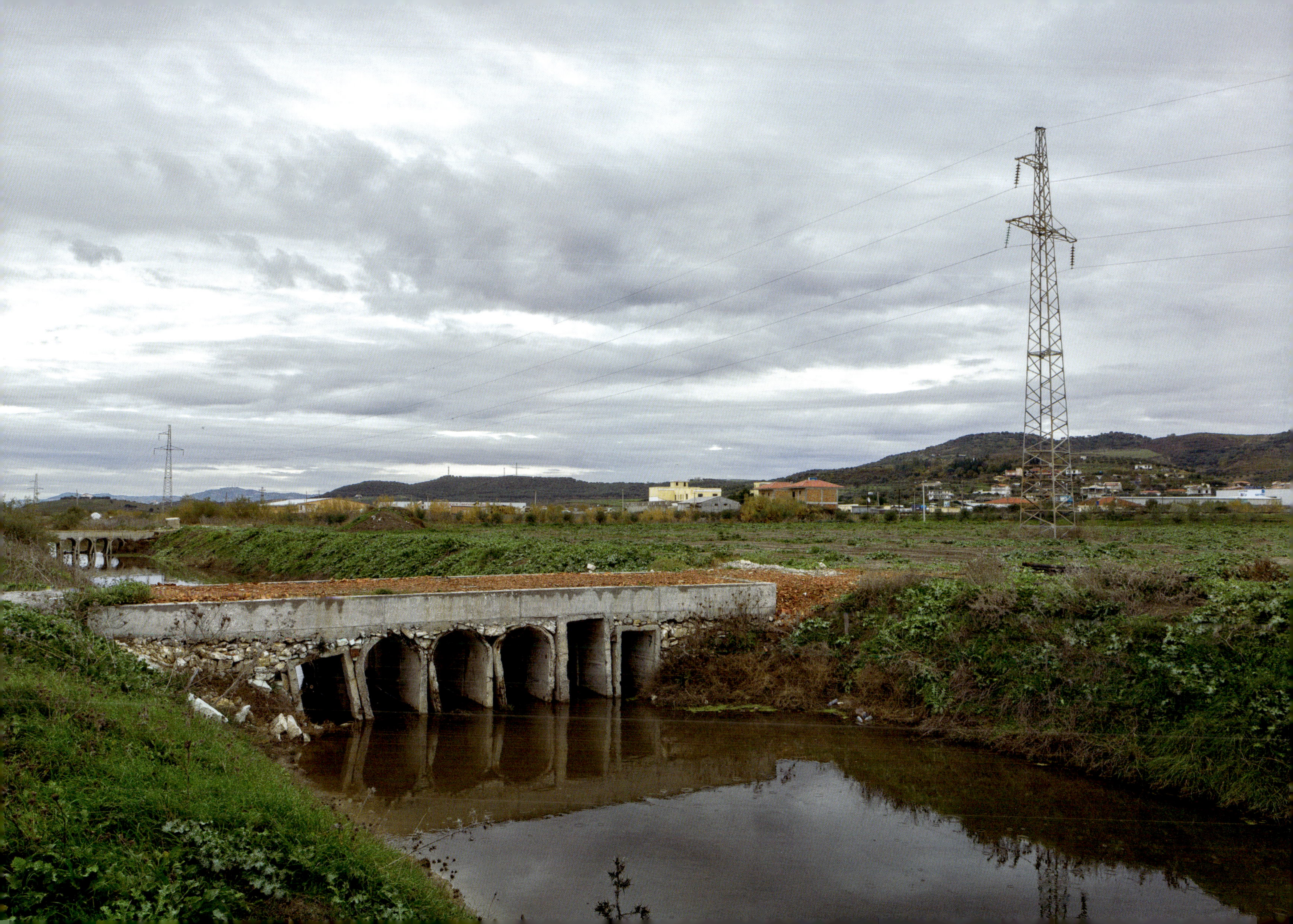

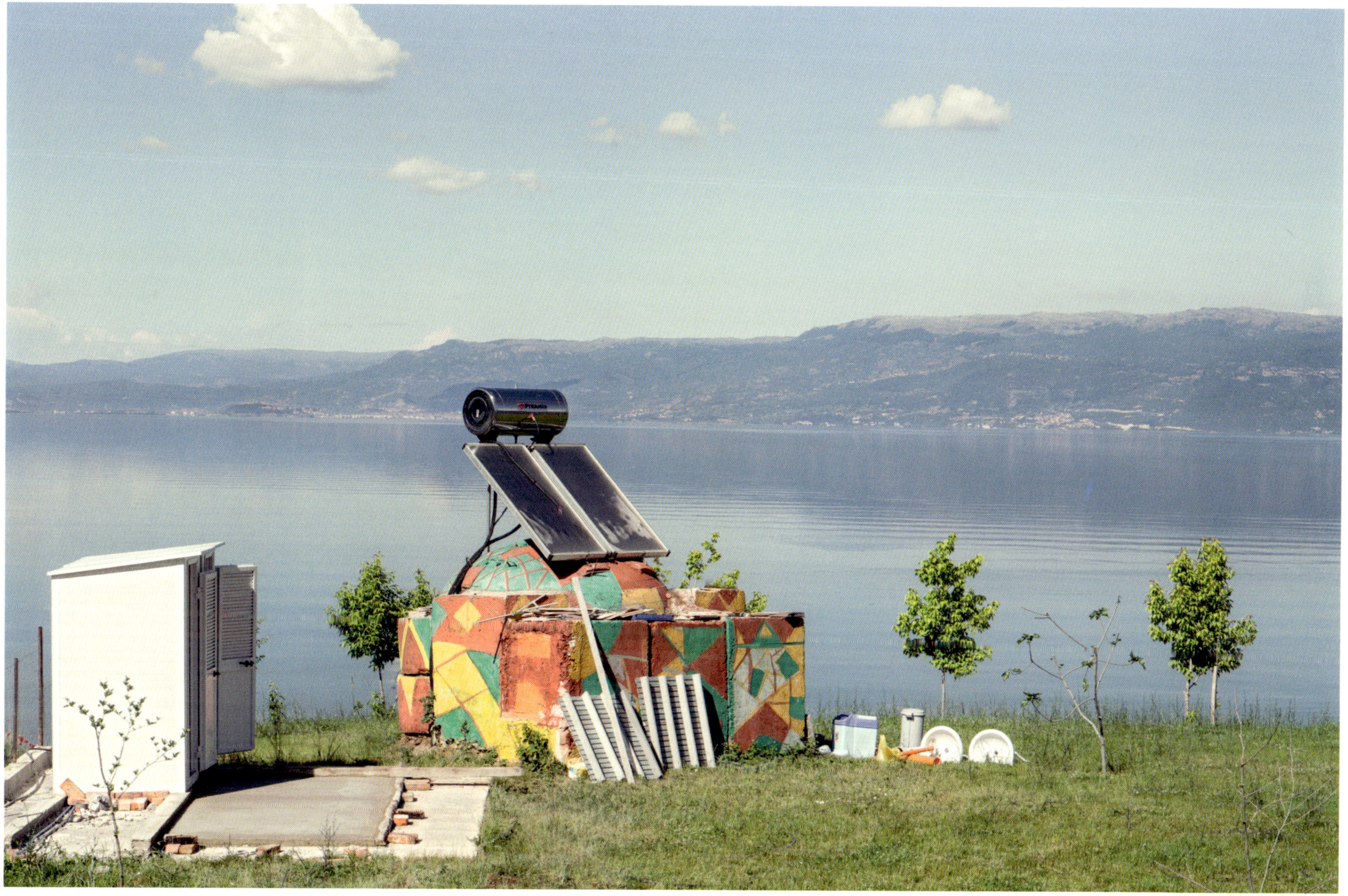

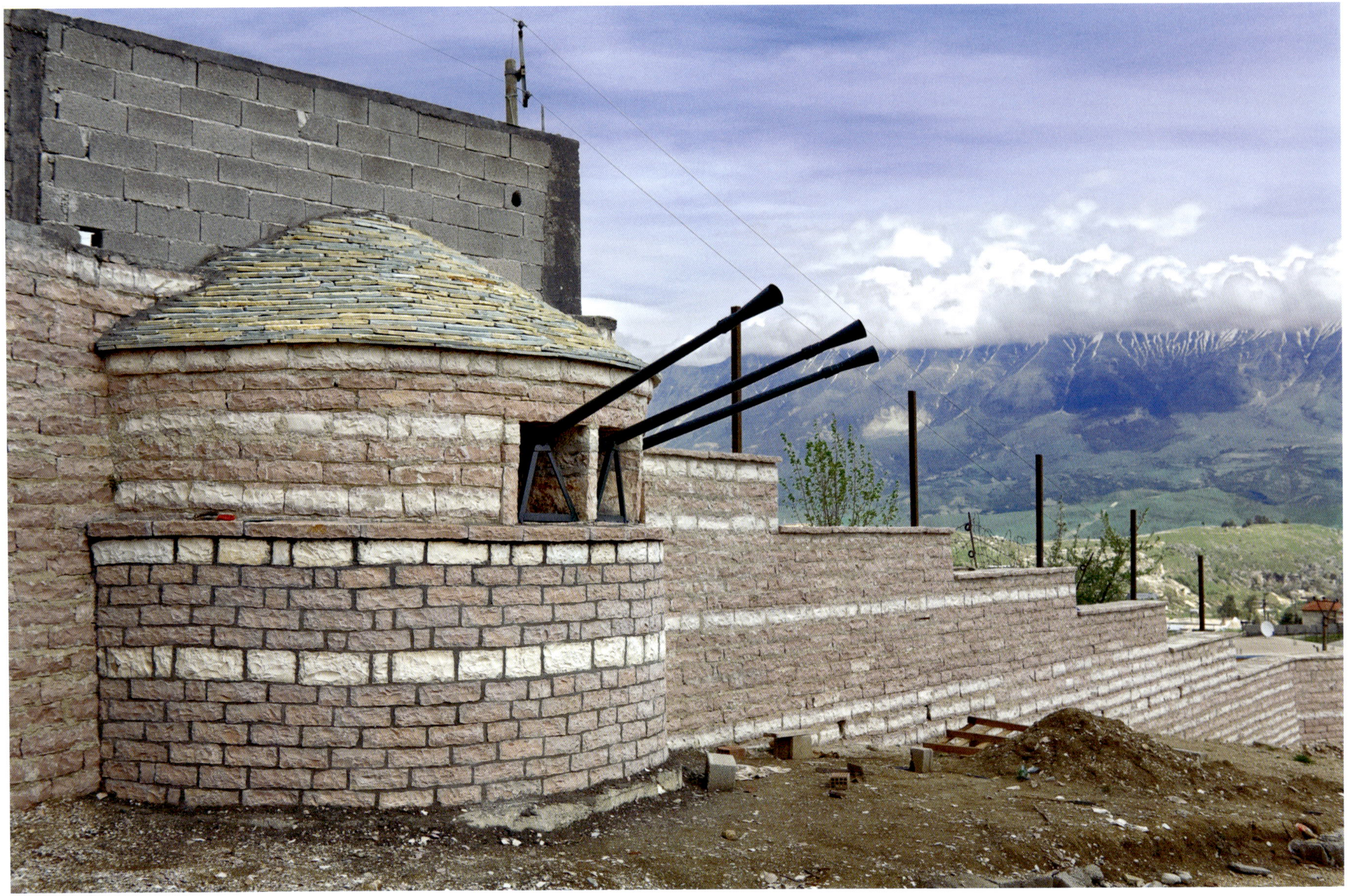

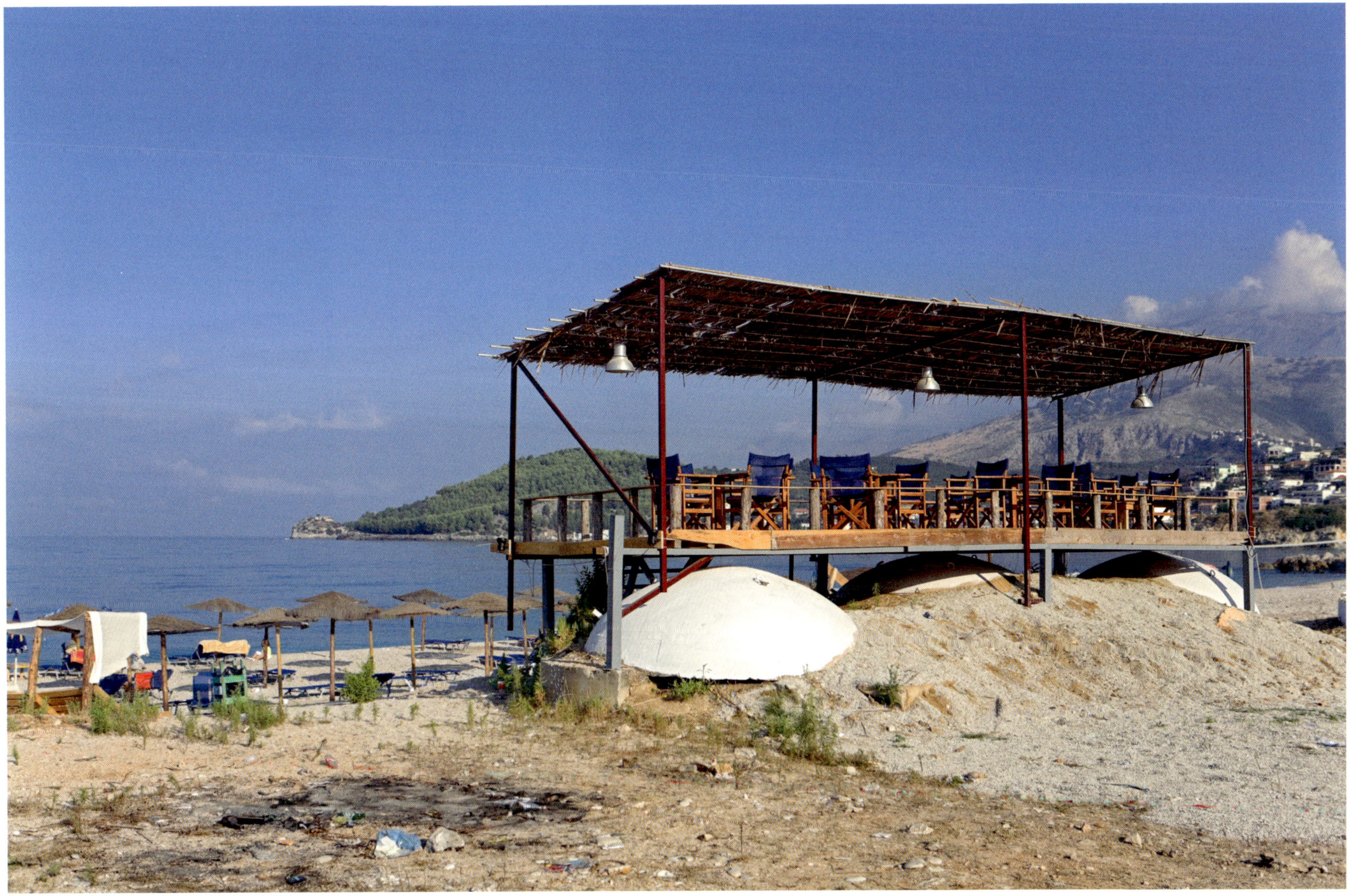

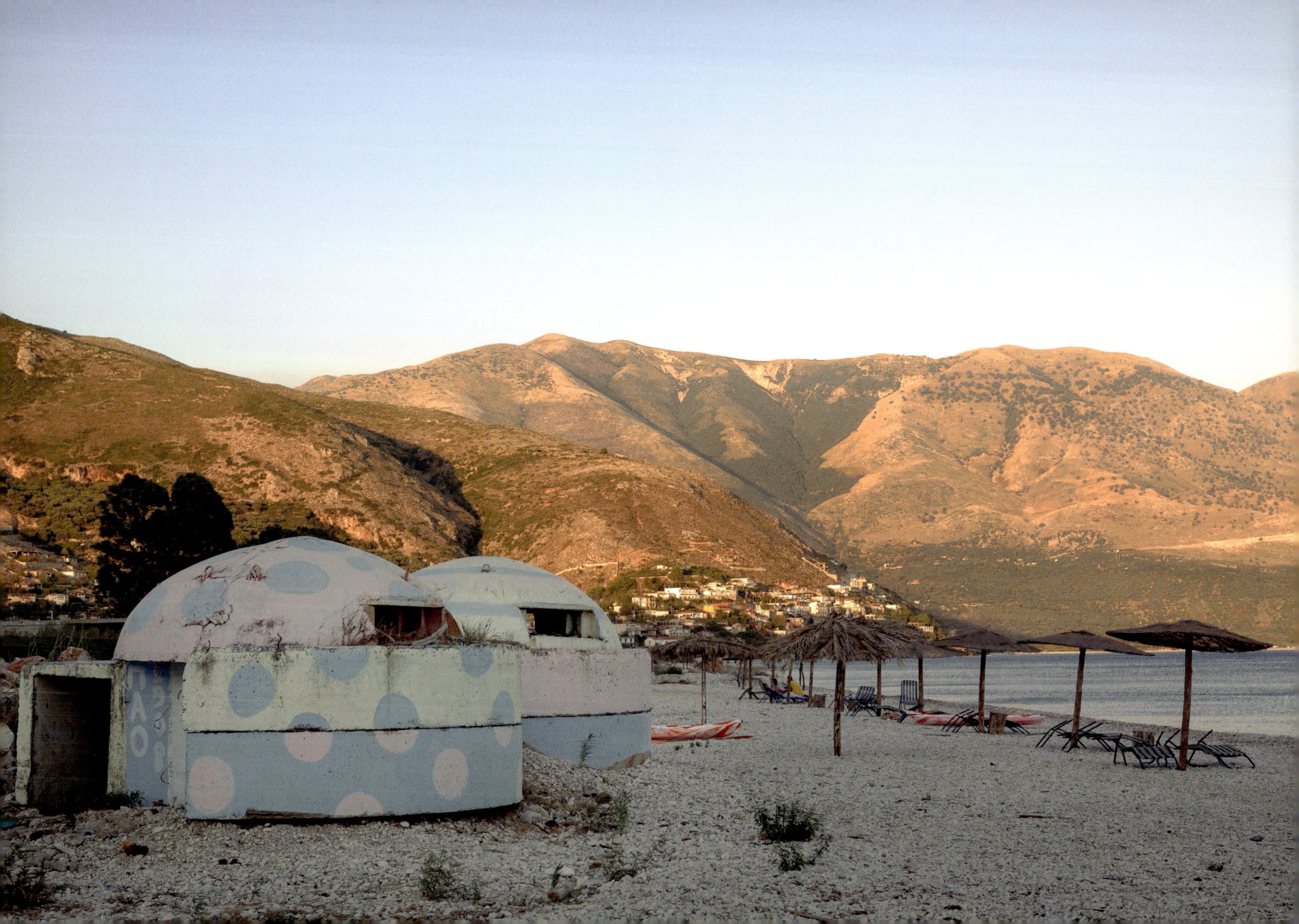

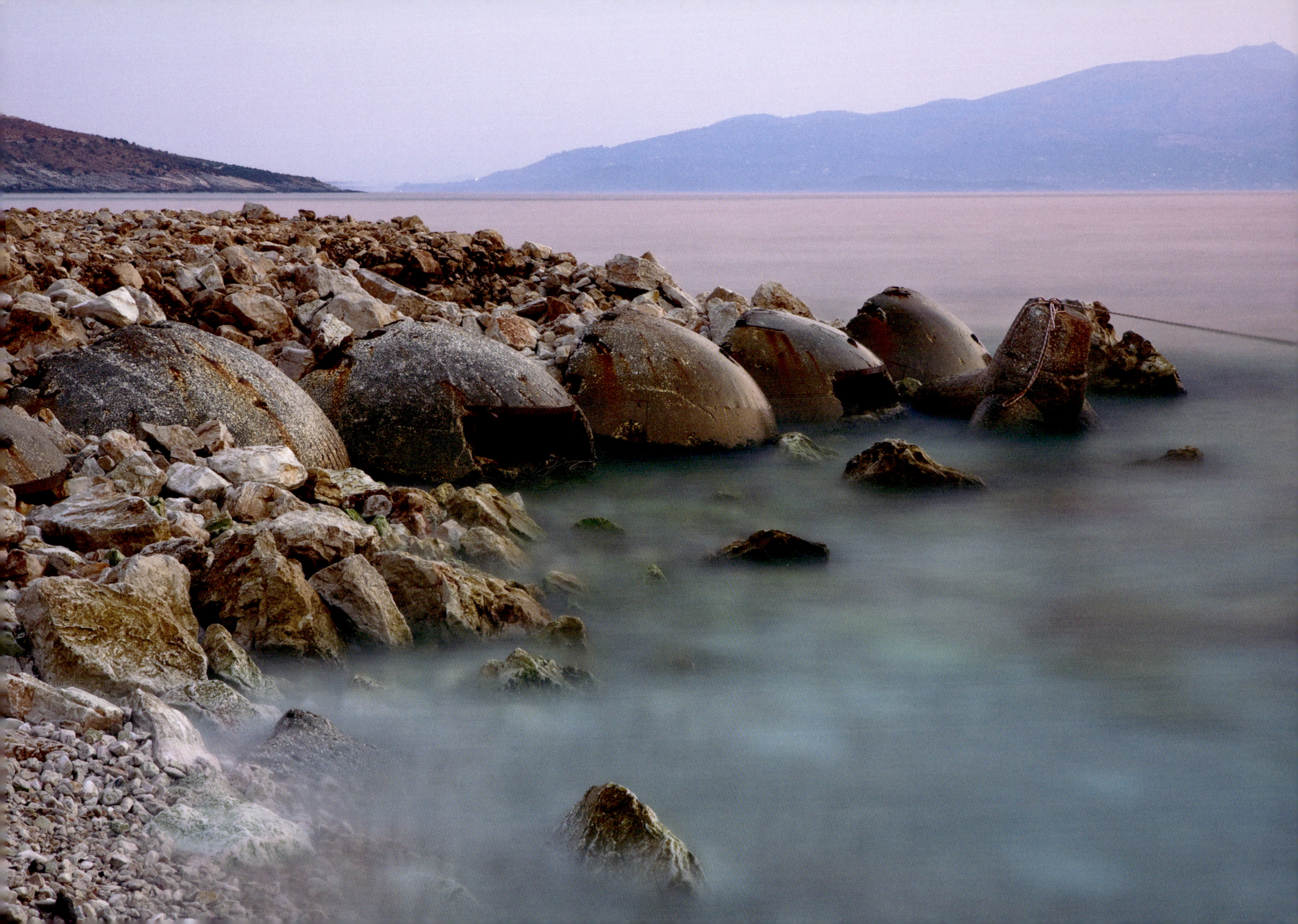

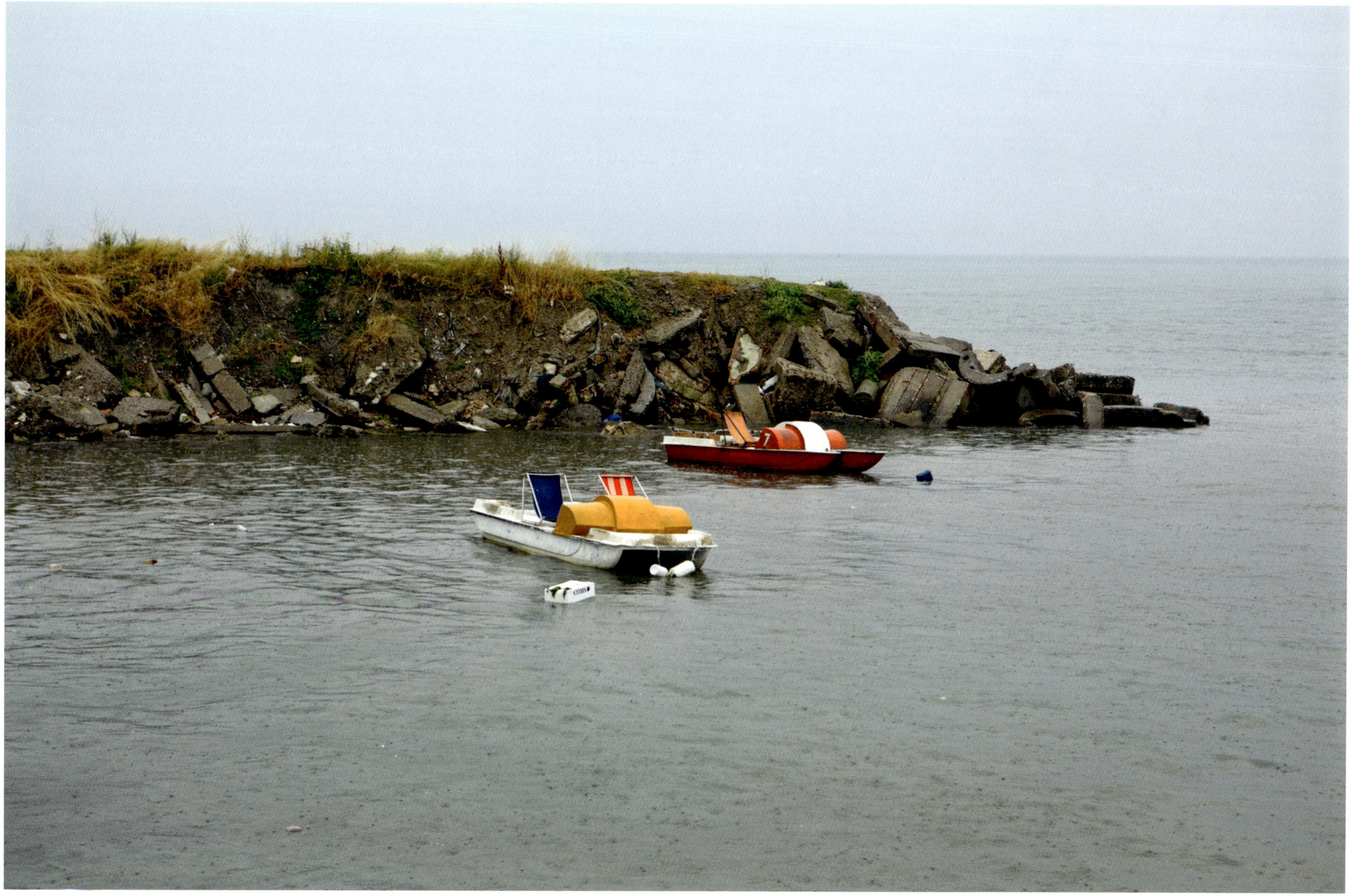

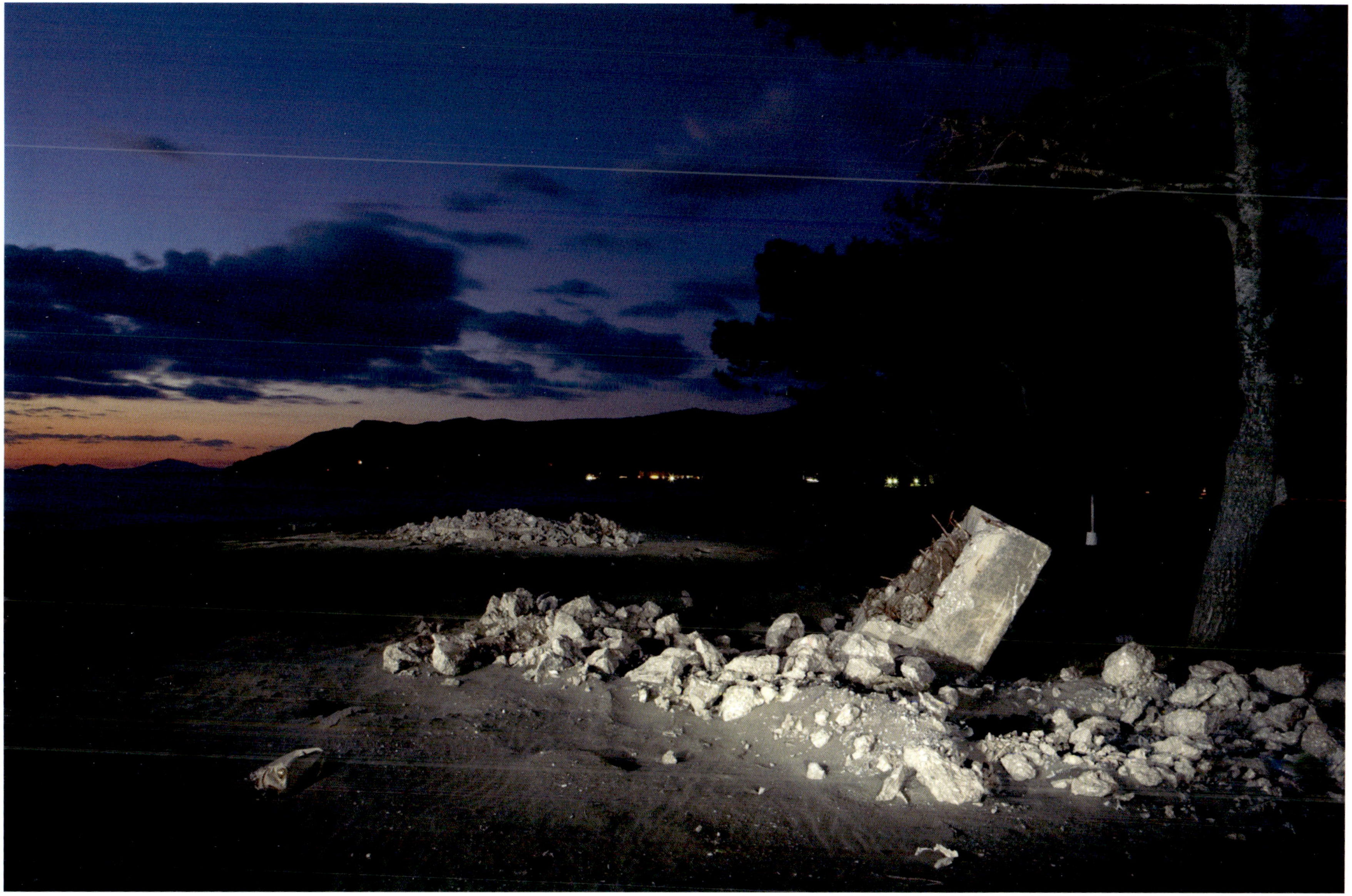

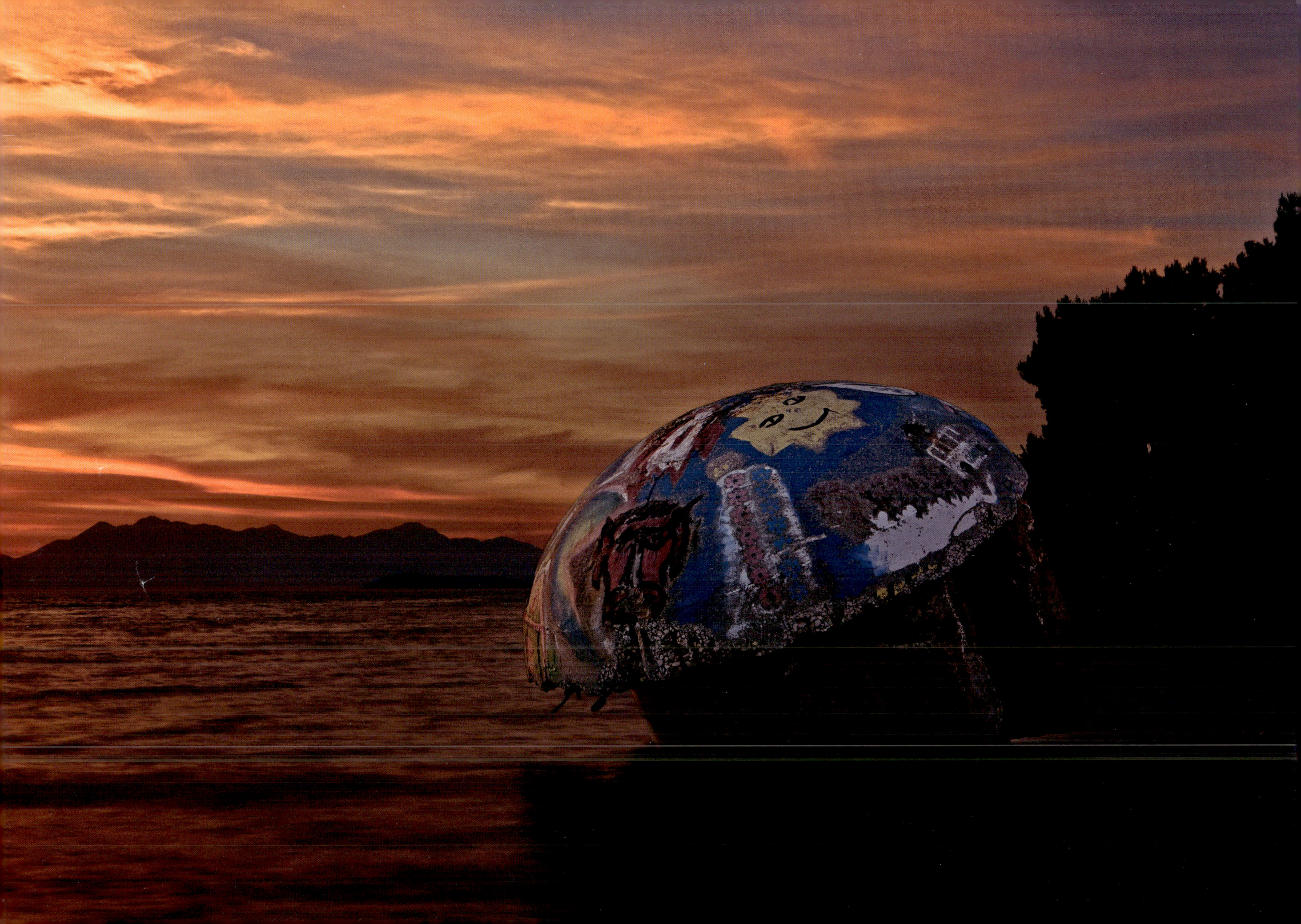

A SHORT HISTORY OF ALBANIA

Albania is a small Balkan country situated on the Adriatic and Ionian coasts, nestled between Greece and Montenegro. Over the past two thousand years it has survived Roman, Norman, Serbian, Ottoman, Italian, and German occupations. But it was a communist dictator, Enver Hoxha, born in the southern Albanian city of Gjirokastër, who was to be one of their harshest oppressors.

All news was controlled by the state, leading the people to believe the outside world wished to invade their communist 'paradise'. Through manipulation and force, the people of Albania toiled with great sacrifice to construct a defence against the 'Imperial' forces and communist revisionists (countries who had altered the Marxist-Leninist doctrine). For this reason the bunkers were built en masse under the Albanian communist leadership. However, they were not built in a day, the process was gradual and the policy took a long time to formulate.

After many years of false starts and factional quarrelling, a unified Albanian Communist party was formed on 8 November 1941 in the capital Tirana. Enver Hoxha was elected secretary and continued to control the party until his death in 1985. In 1944 Albania liberated itself from German occupation and Hoxha seized power, establishing a government in Tirana under Yugoslavian and Soviet tutelage. Relations were eventually broken off with both these important allies. The former in 1948 due to Hoxha's fear of Yugoslavia annexing Albania, and the Soviets in 1961 when Khrushchev adopted communist revisionism. With the Soviet invasion of Czechoslovakia in 1968, Albania withdrew from the Warsaw Pact. Left out in the cold during the Cold War, Hoxha was thrown a political and financial lifeline by the People's Republic of China (PRC) in need of a friendly seat on the United Nations (China's seat was held by The Republic of China, known as Taiwan, until 1971) and an ally in Europe. However this friendship came to an end in 1978 after a